I0569251

SHARDS
OF
LONGING

Poems of Sacred Rupture
& Spoken Healing

Franklyn James

Shards of Longing: Poems of Sacred Rupture and Spoken Healing

Copyright © 2025 by Franklyn James

All rights reserved.

No part of this publication may be reproduced, stored in a retrieval system, or transmitted in any form or by any means, electronic, mechanical, photocopying, recording, or otherwise, without prior written permission from the author or publisher, except for brief quotations used in reviews or critical discussions.

This edition reflects substantial revisions and expansions from earlier versions published in 2022 and 2024.

For permissions, workshops, or communal use inquiries, contact:
https://linktr.ee/franklyn3i

Paperback ISBN: 979-8-218-58602-7
E-book: 979-8-9987699-1-7

For Barbera,
who taught me where home begins.
And to those wandering through memory,
grief, or laughter, may you feel held here.

CONTENTS

9   Introduction

In the Mirror Meeting Myself

Fragments of Us

15   Legacy of the Damned
16   Dark Side of the Rainbow
17   Glimpses from the Abyss
18   The Storm I Was Promised
19   Shadow of the Self
20   You
22   Had I
24   Aging in Riddles
26   Lone Wolf's Lament

Refracted Shards

28   Echoes of the One
30   In His Image, In His Likeness
32   Identity
34   Acceptance
36   Wobniar
40   Epiphany
42   The Tether and the Shackle
44   Half-Lit Truths
46   Socialization

The Worlds Between Us

Voices in the Current

51	Mistakes
52	No Place
54	Love as Infrastructure
57	Rainbow
58	Wrestling with the Alphas
60	A Piece of Pie, Please
62	Free
64	Seduced and Bitten
66	Political Débâcles
69	Quid Pro Quo
70	Monkey Business
73	A Rare Invention
74	Not My Story
76	Turning Tables
78	Decorum or Desire
80	Like Spiders

Scars That Speak

82	In Two Worlds, I Grieve
90	The Touch That Spoke
91	The Moon Within My Scar
92	Negative
95	The Unquiet Soul
98	Positive
100	Things Unsaid
102	A Special Gift
104	The Midas Touch
106	Sensations of Becoming
107	Tender as Thorns
108	Let Go
110	A Peek into the Past
112	Willed into Wakefulness
114	A Lament
115	Cold
116	Killing with Innocence
118	Rejected
119	The Ruin You Left
120	Where I Was Left to Break

121 Words from a Broken Heart
122 A Love Not Mine to Hold
126 No Space Between Us
128 High on Emptiness
130 Wounds Time Cannot Erase
132 Experiencing a Crack Concert
134 Ice

Gathering the Shards

138 The Little Things We Take for Granted
141 Joyful Bitterness
142 In Retrospect: Call, Raise, or Fold
145 Behind the Smile
146 Pause and Ponder
148 A Child's Honor
150 The Other Side
151 Walk
152 Be Positive
154 The Voice of Spring
155 How Things Changed
156 The Rhythms of Nature
158 Holy Intimacy
160 Canvas of Skin
161 Alive
162 Deliberate
164 Answers that Hurt
166 Scars Are Works of Art
168 To Be
169 It Wasn't Mine
170 Kaleidoscope
172 Scars, Sketches, and Scribbles
174 War's Remedy
176 Omariya Finds Peace
178 No Regrets
180 Mi Nah Play Nuh Game
183 Trauma Undone
184 Canticle of Severings
188 Shards of Longing

190 About the Author

INTRODUCTION

Over the years, *Shards of Longing* has undergone significant transformation. What began as fragments of emotion, memory, protest, and prayer has grown into a full-bodied witness of a life lived at the intersections of loss and laughter, silence and song, exile and emergence. This edition, *Shards of Longing: Poems of Sacred Rupture and Spoken Healing*, is the culmination of that journey and a declaration: these are poems meant to be heard as much as read. It is not a tidy account but a final weaving of the raw and the refined, the fractured and the fiercely whole.

The poems gathered here were forged in the crucible of lived experience: cultural dissonance, betrayal, belonging, theological ache, and resilient joy. They do not promise answers. Instead, they bear witness to what often goes unnamed: shame and yearning, reverence and rupture, humor and heartbreak. In doing so, they honor the sacred and difficult work of self-integration.

This is not a linear unfolding. The poems move like breath. They contract, expand, pause, shatter, and restore. Even the punctuation follows this rhythm. Lines begin with a capital letter only when the previous line ends with a period, question mark, or exclamation mark. Otherwise, they continue in lowercase. This deliberate pattern mirrors the work's emotional cadence, capturing both its tension and release—the syntax of the heart.

Rooted in the tradition of dark poetry, the collection does not shy away from existential unease, spiritual dissonance, or emotional shadow. Each section holds its own emotional terrain, with brief invitations to orient the reader. Here, poetry becomes a map, a mirror, a liturgy, and a wound.

The work draws on a range of forms, including Golden Shovel, Sestina, Fibonacci, and prose. The truths they reach for are not fixed but honest, unfinished, and alive. New textures emerge in this complete work: satire beside lament, eros beside friendship, lust beside devotion, tenderness beside critique. These are not separate voices. They are the many observations and selves of one speaker, shaped by fragmentation, identity, and the long labor of becoming whole and carrying what cannot be buried.

You are not required to read this book in order. You may enter wherever your spirit finds an opening. However, should you choose to follow its arc, you will move through a reckoning with the self, a confrontation with the world, and a journey toward a kind of healing that does not erase the wound but gives it voice.

Whether you are returning to these pages or meeting them for the first time, may this collection be a companion. May it help you name what once felt unspeakable. May it be a final benediction of self-acceptance, shaped by fragmentation, identity, and hard-won wholeness, as you navigate your own longing and return.

In the Mirror
Meeting Myself

This section begins with fracture. Here, the poems do not offer resolution but reflection – uncertain, necessary, and raw. These are the moments where the self splinters under the weight of expectation, silence, and inherited shame. The mirror does not lie, but neither does it show the whole. Instead, it distorts, refracts, and challenges the gaze.

In "Fragments of Us," the self is shaped by the world and its labels, rejections, acts of violence, and demands. These poems trace the wounds left by societal scripts, racism, religion, and belonging deferred. In "Refracted Shards," we move inward. What the world breaks, the spirit reclaims piece by piece, through anger, reflection, survival, and sometimes, unspoken tenderness. Together, these poems begin the sacred, uneasy work of seeing the self as it is, unfinished yet still worth meeting.

Fragments of Us

Poems of isolation, rupture, and the uneasy birth of identity amid cultural silence and survival. These are the fragments the world casts off, gathered, held, and spoken.

Legacy of the Damned

In the courts of their hearts, phantoms creep,
hatred rules, and secrets run deep.
The bards in their chambers sing morbid tunes
of roses that bloom on crimson dunes.

In craters they linger; rumors faint and still.
Stories of regrets and horrors that chill.
The fanatic's legacy of disgust and disdain
devours the innocent in its ruthless reign.

Maggots of fanaticism fester and gnaw,
feasting on logic's corpse, their hunger raw.
Heirlooms of chaos their gruesome prize.
In the wake of their obsession, reason dies.

Obsessed, they convene in a fevered trance,
their heritage of bias a lethal lance.
Like telegenic corpses, they parade in pride
and in perverse minds, the truth is denied.

Beware, dear traveler of the damned appetite,
lest the horror of their relics claim you as acolyte.
In secret they conspire, with schemes wild and vile;
a warning to all in each eerie, sinister smile.

Dark Side of the Rainbow

I wandered the streets, a haunting routine
beneath the relentless thrashing of the pouring rain.
Far off motorcars droned and hummed,
sounds mingled with the lonely call of a night train.
Its screech a resonance of a lost refrain.
Behind me, a light pierced the foggy day,
turning raindrops into sparkling tears of light.
I turned and beheld a scene, stark and strange;
ashen skies weakened the rainbow's promise.
Yet inverted colors, a range of mood and radiance,
bathed me in hues of bruised pink,
an allure to stormy longings, yearning to unfurl.
Lured to the threshold of passion withheld,
and subdued by its purplish ink,
a flood of emotions turned my world upside down.
The taste of night's flirtation with frustration.
"Wobniar!" I cried, its name a reversed incantation.
It replied, "Fear not, lonely one, accept my aberration."
Perplexed, I fled the confrontation,
waking to a world split by lightning's whip.
The skies roared as clouds were torn asunder
revealing a hallowed space in the heavens.
In awe, I gazed, my mind spinning; I was shaken.
I beheld the other side of the rainbow's face,
where light and darkness meet,
dreams and reality unravel,
and mysteries remain obscured, undecoded.

Glimpses from the Abyss

Lost
souls
in despair.
In unknown lands,
spirits wail, bodies in limbo,
skins scorned, genders obscured, attracting reproach and praise.
With vision compromised, we see only conflicts, and diversity's cruel blade severing hope,
forging divisions in dungeons of delusion. While from gloom a weak whisper rises,
echoes of unity, for kinship outside forsaken places,
where souls, tarnished and wandering,
also seek forgiveness.
Yet bound
hopelessly,
unendingly.

The Storm I Was Promised

A creature of catastrophe, a harbinger of fright.
It emerges, a swirling vortex reigning in chaos,
assaulting with wind, mist, and dust.
Dark-white, it engulfs all in utter obscurity.
From this disorder, a dismal form arises.
Transfixed, I watch as it ruthlessly attacks,
piercing the air with a feverish howl.

Helpless, hapless, I—
I am caught in its menacing sway.
By fate's cruel twist, my afflictions anchor me.
I stare into the face of death;
my spine shudders, then freezes.
In this ill-omened revelation,
will it be said, "He met his end?"

Like the sound of a thousand horses galloping,
like the wailing of vengeful banshees,
a voice thunders at me.
From this clouded mist,
this dust-filled cyclonic cauldron,
a chilling truth emerges:
the life I lead is veiled in chaos,
before the blessings hidden in its folds appear.

Shadow of the Self

In the mirror's gaze, I meet a bleak reflection,
a silhouette stripped of all connection.
Am I an echo in someone's memory,
or a specter summoned by sorcery?

Longing to be seen, I roam in the dark,
seeking identity, a defining mark.
Eclipsed by doubt, wrapped in mystery.
Am I merely a question in my own history?
It is within this abyss that I strive to find
the essence of me, beneath the outline.

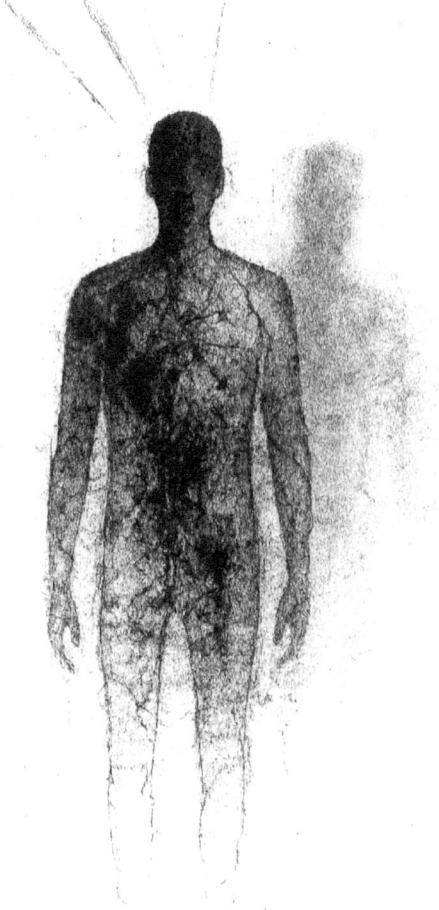

You

What do you know, and what have you seen?
Have you seen a person whose meal is *refuse*?
Do you know the weight of the pain I bear?
Have you prayed for healing in anguish and tears,
yet all you receive is sheer aggravation,
the constant pulse of life's provocation?
In all of this, I'm haunted by memories of You.

What have you seen, and what do you know?
Have you lived in a house where the ceiling leaks,
eaten your meals bland and unseasoned?
Have you walked bare, unshod and unseen;
at home, in classrooms, even in cathedrals?
In those days, I didn't know You.

What do you know, and what have you seen?
Have you carried burdens that crush your soul
while laughter surrounds you, careless and cold?
Have you trusted in silence, your heart keeping score,
only to feel hollowed inside, desiring life no more?
In your absence, I sought a sign from You.

What have you seen, and what do you know?
Alive, yet each breath feels like constant pain,
toiling without rest as debt tightens like knots.
Have you studied in a world that's collapsing,
sought peace in faith, but found a battlefield instead,
met with contempt, scheming, and scorn?

What do you know, and what have you seen?
For even in chaos, one may find truth;
in life's madness, seek and uncover meaning.
The harvest of my trials and tests,
twisted relations and empathy strained,
is wisdom born from the ashes of decay.
My tears, once steeped in grief and rue,
now bear the bittersweet trace of You.

Had I

Here, in anguish, my mind is a river I wade into slowly;
I sit, besieged by life's cruel parody.
Tormented sighs, a ghostly choir leaks from my lips.
I savor a foreboding fear
and feel the ache in places relief dares not tread.
It sears; a sinister fire, fear's icy fingers
tracing a path along my spine.
A furnace ignites deep in my chest.
Dark, consuming, its heat engulfing my being.
The *soreness, and sourness*, residue of secrets long buried,
claw at my throat, a trolling tormentor,
poised to rip the life from my withering frame.

Inside this storm, where weeping brews and rages,
the wind speaks in tongues with the trees.
Its laughter—ghostly, mocking, transient, cold—
derides me, then hurries away.
My soul, knotted in affliction and woe,
watches the chilling waltz of wind and leaves—spellbound.
From east to west, a gust surges, a tempestuous tide
bearing leaves and the remains of forgotten debris.
In it, I hear the cries of the departed.
The leaves float like the souls of the lost,
a spectral procession, transient and forlorn;
a vision of dread, sending shivers to my bones.
This unholy communion of wind and leaves,
a grim omen at the witching hour of midday.
Gone are my days of peace,
lost in a maze of longing.

Had I witnessed this dark spectacle before,
the wind and leaves, in their deathly swirl,
a sublime display of nature's wrathful splendor.
Had I felt their passionate touch;
reminiscent of the deluges of Noah's days,
the dread of divine wrath would vanish,
and I would realize His provision for humanity.

Had I felt the wind's gentle caress;
its dance with leaves, a wild race in the garden,
then, in my heart, a thrill of wonder would awaken
memories of Elijah's flight to Horeb.
I would have heard the Divine's whisper, clear and faint,
kindling a fire within my spirit.

Had I beheld this wondrous scene;
wind and leaves playing a mischievous symphony,
sending both young and old into a frenzy of delight,
who, in a chorus of shrieks, skip a frantic ballet to shelter.
I would have basked in the humor of their frolic.

In my youth, such a display of nature's whimsy
would have been a comforting visit,
a manifestation to soothe my restless spirit.

Now, this miracle, modest yet majestically fearful,
floods my being with hope and dread.
My tears stream down, carving rivers of anguish.
In time, will these visions, once harbingers of fear,
become wells of renewal, bathing my soul
in their radiant brilliance?

Aging in Riddles

I brood over the words of Qoheleth;
perplexing and more chilling than amusing.
My mind, being what it is, sees varied allusions,
some not particularly helpful.
Is it nature's impulse or the gods' decrees
that give life authenticity and meaning?

The saying about life's journey feels tragic.
"Life under the sun": such a peculiar phrase.
The antithesis and remedy proposed
for human existence extends beyond worldly living,
centering instead on reverence for the Divine.

The idea that young people abhor eternity
and anything sacred is fundamentally flawed.
It is a slander of the juvenile that fits the adult best.
Or perhaps it holds a little truth for both;
a mystery for time to expose.

Who can decode these obscured speeches?
Keepers of houses shudder;
the once upright and strong stoop.
The few grinders left stopped working.
Birds' songs grow faint,
doors to the streets are shut,
and fear of heights arises.
The almond tree blossoms,
silver cords snap,
and golden bowls are broken.

In this cryptic speech, the meaning is quite plain:
shivering bodies, loss of teeth, sight, and hearing;
hair turns gray, and the body wrinkles
a tactful way of saying, "old and decrepit."
This reversal of youth, does it have a remedy?
To answer might be petrifying, the evidence
inspiring and sometimes spine-tingling.

The simplest joys grow heavy, like burdens of stone.
Some—who? become nuisances,
hidden away for reasons of vice or virtues misplaced.

I contemplate the poet's words,
mysterious, amusing, and outright alarming.
And my mind, as it is, sees many assumptions
for life under the sun, finding more paradoxes
than solutions.

Lone Wolf's Lament

Like a lone wolf howling beneath a crescent moon,
a lone silhouette against a starless dune
I stand, an emblem of solitude, my cry a mournful tune,
beneath a brooding sky and a world blind to its doom.

I yearn for the pack, for connections to root and bloom,
but I am wrapped in darkness, sealed in a dense cocoon.
In this bone-white dusk, my heart rivals a monsoon,
aching for a companion to escape this marooned gloom.

Refracted Shards

Poems of inner reckoning, spiritual residue,
and the labor of becoming. Here, the self
returns to itself through memory, tension,
and the slow naming of truth.

Echoes of the One

What wisdom shaped this living thread
from clay and nerve to soul and dread?
Systems, organs, tendons, and nerves
bound in harmony that tirelessly serve.
Blood flows in cycles, from right to left,
guided by the heart, a deft architect.

Skins of ash, amber, oiled mahogany blend,
a palette of life that knows no end.
Like you, I drift in twilight's gleam;
like me, you're caught in a bizarre dream.
The North's cold cliffs, the South's warm sand,
from East to West, under the moon's command,
where borders blur, and cultures align,
our values weave like creeping vines.

Wealth and want walk side by side
on life's strange stage, where follies hide.
Each person takes part in this spectral art.
In shaping our lives, we all play a part.
Every soul seeks a safe place to belong,
to weather existence's chilling song,
to touch the void, feel what's unseen,
perhaps understand what the shadows mean.

We sense a world foreboding, morose,
with odors of a past, too close, too gross.
Yet, in this shared tune, we're bound as one;
the same design, under the same sun.
Through every crisis, each daunting grief,
in the *Lover's* care, sorrows find relief.

Connectedness to otherness, a trait all share,
reaching for what lies beyond our sphere.
Some seek it in ideas, others in idols they trade,
in the creations they've mined or made.
In the stillness, where God seems gone,
they search within for the will to go on.

Those marked by the sacred seal of eternity
bear signs of the One crowned in humility.
And through the pain where anguish speaks,
we find in Christ what the broken seek.

In His Image, In His Likeness

If you are confused, it is because i am.
In a maze of thought, i am lost, found, then wander
through life's womb, where the Divine's heart pulses.
In this abysmal state, my quest to fathom the I AM
breeds frustration in a mind created finite.

God is Spirit! The breath on the burning bush;
beyond flesh, beyond bone, beyond fields of forms.
From the heart of chaos, He illuminates our minds.
Omnipotent, Omniscient, the eternal light.
Omnipresent in the hushed obscurity
woven through the strands of space and time.

The I AM is not as i am.
Mere dust in time's brief breath,
bound to the ticking of a transient clock.
God's acts of creating, caring, and reclaiming the lost
reveal Him as the architect of order,
whose image is cast across our human borders.

The sexes were made in God's image and likeness;
from them, our genders are shaped and named.
To shape, to tend, to walk in sacred dignity.
Not bound by flesh, God transcends mortal forms.
A fortress is He: fearsome and kind, a divine paradox.

A just judge in the mind's dark court, God rules with justice.
Compassionate and present at the threshold of our days.
Slow to anger.
Love without measure.
Like stars in their courses:
silent, steady, secure.

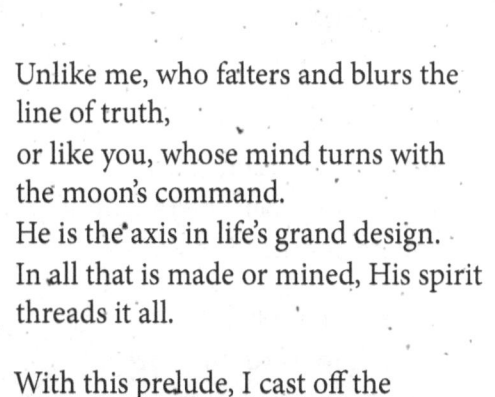

Unlike me, who falters and blurs the
line of truth,
or like you, whose mind turns with
the moon's command.
He is the axis in life's grand design.
In all that is made or mined, His spirit
threads it all.

With this prelude, I cast off the
vestiges of doubt,
to clear the fog of who i am, who you
are, and I AM.

Identity

I am what society's mirrors reflect:
a shape-shifter in its dystopic context.
A man, a woman, a child, a shade,
an age, a stage, a role self-made.

I am the labels hung upon my frame:
married, single, a story of blame.
A sibling, a parent, or one estranged,
bound by blood or labels prearranged.

I am the color adorning my skin:
brown, ebony, ivory, and the stories within.
I am a worker, a dreamer, a banished alien,
with no place, and no one, in all creation.

I am the product of the faith I keep:
spiritual, devout, with roots running deep.
Defined by the deeds I sow and reap,
steady in storms where doubters weep.

I am the love that dares not speak:
straight, queer, broken but not weak.
A thinker, a learner; wisdom I seek
in the calls of the ancient and oblique.

Tall or short, within the flesh's span,
judged ugly or lovely, outside the clan.
In the mirror's gaze, I see the ban,
the hurt of a soul seen as less or more than.

Please stop! Reflect and see me clear.
Look beyond the label, the doubt, and fear.
I wrote "I AM" to erase the smear
in the somber trace of a single tear.

I pen these lines, a soul's dark chant,
in my declining years, a poet's rant.
From the depths of my being, a truth I grant
and sadly whisper, "I am what I can't."

I write my prose in pain's iron grasp;
yet my voice will roar despite its clasp.
In the raw, unspoken truth of a bleeding pen,
I ask, "Who are we?" of the strangers within,
and despite its chains, the soul cries, "I am …"

Acceptance

In the mirror's face, where fantasy parodies reality,
I try to forge connection in a maze of confusion.
Eyes wide open, yet I am lost in a dream,
I wrestle with the essence of human tolerance.
Is there meaning, when understanding is a lost art,
in a world where acceptance is hard to achieve?

Is harmony with every soul so hard to achieve?
And what of accepting another's spiritual reality?
To pledge no creed yet honor all is a fine art,
while empathy's path is riddled with confusion.
Still, we wrestle with the paradox of tolerance,
an enigma at the heart of our collective dream.

From despair's abyss, I drift through a moonless dream.
My heart stirs, a foretaste of what we might achieve.
It beats to the rhythm of troubled tolerance,
haunted by unresolved rhetoric—a catch-22 in reality.
Through catacombs carved in tenebrous confusion,
our quest to belong is hindered by fear's cruel art.

There's beauty in this strange, demanding, dark art,
even as our ideals and affections dissolve into dreams.
Sifting through shards of the past may ease confusion
when acceptance is a possibility we cannot achieve.
Out of this nightmare, understanding tests our reality
as frayed emotions dangle from fragile tolerance.

A measure of understanding weighs the rules of tolerance.
True tolerance; embracing even intolerance is life's sly art.
It cannot be discarded without distorting reality:
our values slipping away like visions after dreams,
leaving us to wonder what we ever hoped to achieve,
spiraling once more into brutal confusion.

And so, are we left to wander through this confusion;
no covenant to bind us, to foster tolerance?
The goal, acceptance, we may yet achieve
as we paint our destiny. I call it beauty, we call it art.
Or will it remain beyond our dreams,
wedged on the mirrored edge of reality?

Reality or illusion, we still seek to achieve
some measure of acceptance within the confusion,
where dreams of tolerance rest in the art of understanding.

Wobniar

A flawless curve, suspended in the serene sky.
Fastened by nothing, yet stitching sky to soil.
Half-born of shadow, half of burning light,
it rises where the Earth kisses the rain.
Each droplet, cupped by the sun, is a lens of wonder.

Of the seven shades, color personified,
is there one most prominent, a natural divide?
A boundary in the prismatic spectrum of humans?
Not only does the sun provide infinite shade,
it sustains the melanin of the skin.

Skins glorified, yet tabooed, reflect an upside-down,
inside-out world, creating alienation and doubt.
Conformity and individuality are in constant battle.
There are indeed people of color,
but how can we assume who fits where?

The memory that certain skin is deemed evil lingers.
Black is burdened with meanings, diabolic and dark,
a reminder of our past, it speaks of our ancestors' days.
They say it is the absence of light,
not found in anything. It can only be missing.

The rainbow or *Wobniar* derides the color that's denied.
Black is used to describe all that scares:
$$\text{demons,}$$
$$\text{death,}$$
$$\text{diabolism.}$$

It becomes something to fear.
A mystery,
veiled in delusion,
weighed down by heaviness,
filled with grief,
depression,
and rebellion.

Social narratives used Black to categorize and other.
We are Black—yet called "colored." What a paradox.
Placed in a box with those not born to this identity.
History reminds us that we weren't fully human.
Three-fifths of a person.
Has the rest ever been restored?

Is Black found in any color of the rainbow?
Still, it bears a meaning all its own,
imbued with beauty, power, status, and elegance.
It hides things and absorbs the stains of pain.

When Black skin is soaked in blood, hate
and conflict. The enemy cannot see;
their torment finds no purchase there.
Loved ones think our skin is drenched with water,
but it holds what they'll never know.

Black absorbs light, warmth, and history.
Leveraged in headlines, politics, and markets.
An identity fetishized, distorted, commodified,
Carrying mystery and beauty from which *Wobniar* is born.
Know this! We are not confined to the skin we wear.

Black allows others to stand out, but many deny this
wanting to see life in simpler terms.
It's black or white.
Ancient customs crown white as beauty's frame,
the canvas for rainbows,
while Black is deemed the opposite,
left out of the spectrum.

This binary contains a restless tension:
a game of the visible against the invisible,
of linguistics and semantics,
a tango of politics, language, and power.
While we lament this tired logic,
there is another way: rainbow thinking.

This opens a spectrum of options,
a world where truth resists division.
It sees nuance where others draw hard lines,
yet even here, a question remains.
A color missing from the arc.
A voice long absent from the chorus.
It is Black.
Unless, somewhere,
there is a Wobniar.

Epiphany

A vision falls like dust on untainted water,
its weight a gathering of stones in my mind's eye.
A wheel turns within a wheel's embrace,
alive with fire that spills beyond its reach.
Blazing and swirling, a whirlwind of energy,
a force neither time nor space can bind.

A fire of knowing; consuming, revealing,
where faith and fate collide in a cosmic clash,
piercing the air, fierce and confounding,
summoning warmly, yet clearly warning.
Unfathomable, splendid, terrifying in beauty,
it draws me closer, and I step forward,
glimpsing the edges of my tomorrow.

I see a vessel; empty, yet full,
waiting to hold what words cannot capture.
Pulsing and pausing in a rhythm I know:
of light and shadow, life and death.
The disclosure lands, raw as fresh wounds,
carved from the bowels of waiting worlds.
I tread slowly as it brushes my thoughts.

A sound stirs, swelling the air, a primal hum,
the pulse of countless hearts beating in tune,
roaring like distant, thundering waterfalls.
I stand, suspended, on the edge of knowing.

Alas! To know is not to be!
A glimpse of reality, now veiled in the haze.
For as much as is shown, as much is concealed.
As the vision fades, a throne takes its place,
crafted from the Earth's rarest gems,
shining with beauty beyond telling,
like thousands of rain-kissed petals.
This sound, both terrifying and mystical,
weakens my knees and rings with affirmation.

A thunderclap of truth surges through the mist,
a fierce baptism of understanding.
My life opens before me, a sign of tragedy to come:
pain preceding joy, wisdom its reward,
a love that binds to the destiny ahead.
This insight, laced with fibers of tears and fire,
pulls at the fabric of my soul's deepest desires,
revealing as much as it conceals;
a mystery eternal, without start or end.

The Tether and the Shackle

I thought we were friends,
bound by the tether of time,
sharing joy, immersed in laughter.
But I glimpsed your decadence,
obscured in ambiguity and artistry.
Was this divorce by choice or by chance?
I pondered the cause.
You professed our deep bond
yet drifted like smoke in the wind,
adorned in an armor of deceit and disguise.
When your façade began to crumble,
deception snarled, baring jagged teeth.
Your fascination with my authenticity
is cloaked in ulterior aims.
To me, you were a friend; to you, I was a pawn,
a chess piece in the sinister game you played.

I watched as you unraveled,
haunted by demons you harbored,
teetering on the brink of insanity.
I pleaded, "Face your truth—I'll stand by you."
Yet pride had bound you tightly in its shackles,
or was it shame that chained your heart?
You would not turn to face the self within,
hiding from the truth you feared to know.
Even if only in isolation's cell,
the inescapable truth will find you.
I told you all along. I know why.

I cast words like seeds, prayers for awakening,
hoping they'd yield courage within you.
In life's myriad options, wisdom holds the key,
for no one can unlock your destiny.
Destiny is forged by the choices we make,
and fate is shaped by intentional actions,
not by mere chance or accident.
Confined thoughts become a prisoner's plight.
Buried feelings are a tempest brewing.
Repressed actions, a ticking time bomb,
shattering the psyche in a mournful display.

Mere pills cannot quell the mind's affliction.
True healing lies in self-acceptance.
It rests in knowing your heart's truth,
believing in yourself, and finding your why.

Half-Lit Truths

In this age of moral ambiguity and distorted virtues,
right and wrong are bound like twisted ropes.
Information flows like a murky river,
and lies writhe like serpents in an Alabaster sea.
Is it true: to know is to fall, but to fall is to grow?
"In the tempest's fury, do not forsake the vessel,
for the winds heed not your command,"
warns the night in its cold, callous rhapsody.

"Not lacking in character," we assert,
floating in a world of half-truths,
where polluted streams carry distorted dreams,
and sacred texts bend to selfish schemes.
Does not progress rise from conformity's ashes?
To question is to disrupt the script of power,
for nothing in this masquerade is as it seems.

"Not without its charm," we say, averting our eyes.
In an age of superficiality, expression is stifled,
and honesty bends into something unrecognizable.
Freedoms taste sweet but carry the sting of exile.
Obedience is praised, yet curiosity births division,
for Adam watched, but Eve dared.
Pride parades, veiled in a guise of virtue,
blinded by illusions, unaware of its fall.

"It's not that I don't care; it's complicated," we claim.
While truth cries "Day!" our lies insist "Night."
In a fog of choices, right is wrong and wrong is gospel,
a personal, tormenting war in every heart,
clinging to a transient life as if it could ever be enough.
Rebellion drums in the hollow of the human condition.
Yet in this dance of darkness and refracted light,
lies a truth too stark, too raw for mortal minds.

"It has a certain *je ne sais quoi*," we concede,
as ambiguity and ambivalence anchor our arguments.
In a world where hypocrisy is clandestine currency,
we veil ourselves in civility and double standards.
We cradle flames we know will scorch us,
yet cannot summon the will to snuff them out.
God's silence echoes louder than a serpent's words
while our lives remain a performance,
a carefully rehearsed illusion.

"It's not my place to say. Please reconsider," we caution,
recalling how the fruit first taught us doubt,
to question the hands that feed.
In the turmoil of our own minds, we drift,
clinging to wreckage in a fog of moral despair.
The Divine calls us to a higher purpose,
yet we remain adrift in a turbulent sea of ambiguity.
Truth burns brighter than stupor, leaving its scars
and if the forbidden fruit was bitter, ignorance is worse.

Socialization

It rests on this notion: internalization.
Even the dismal stitched their lessons into us;
diabolic habits shared across tables and time.
Carved from a medley of thoughts and grim realities,
behaviors crafted and sustained mock both fool and sage.

When attitudes are forged through pain and discord,
we solemnly vow not to pass these vices on,
nor engage in disputes from dusk until dawn,
but to open our eyes to the plight of others.
We promise to speak the language of love, not of war.
But isn't it ironic how we condone the things we condemn?

Traditions. Dialects. Ideologies.
What once shaped identity now bears despair.
They include loathing the virtuous, embracing the vile.
Do yesterday's chains outlast today's winds of change?
We plead, "Help us, O God, not to multiply injuries
or make them part of our destinies."

Even though the cage is gilded, its bars remain.
A pattern we inherit, thread by thread.
Is it not a charade to treasure what corrupts?
Venomous words once hurled at us,
now wielded against others to harm and divide,
to confound and perplex?

Opinions and trends, faithless companions by our side.
In them, we were born, socialized, and taught.
So, do not expect me to change from the start.
For all my days were drenched in strife;
I quarreled and fought with every soul I crossed.

What was inflicted upon me, I pass on with ease.
What was done to me, I replicate without thought.
Do not hold me accountable for deeds I performed;
they are the legacy I inherited, gifts from my environment.

A fool's defiance echoes through every age.
I cannot force anyone to heal or change.
They will learn from their teachers: agony and anguish,
in the company of the forsaken.

Cruel lessons learned must be painfully unlearned,
shedding what burdens the soul, piece by piece.
Be it fashion or trend, wealth or companions,
we must confront our hatred and nurture what is good,
or risk the soul withering from neglect.

Socialization molds us for better or worse.
It shapes our tongues, tempers, and truths over time.
It teaches us to speak before we know our voice,
to follow paths carved by others' hands.

If we do not question what we inherit,
we risk becoming prisoners of a flawed design.
The world is a web we each help to weave;
if one thread is corrupted, the tapestry grieves.
Let our actions rewrite the lessons we've learned
so those who come after us inherit something whole.

The Worlds Between Us

This section shifts outward, into the terrain of relationship, resistance, and society. These poems confront injustice, desire, and grief not only as internal states but also as conditions shaped by systems of power. What happens when longing is met with silence? When faith becomes exclusion? When sexuality and Blackness are othered, fetishized, or denied belonging? These poems answer through confrontation and catharsis, refusal and reclamation.

Yet this is also a section of connection, navigating love, trauma, sexuality, and memory with unflinching vulnerability. Whether recounting political tensions, fractured relationships, or intimate violence, these works refuse simplicity. They move between the sacred and the sensual, the societal and the personal.

In Two Worlds, I Grieve finds its home here as both anchor and elegy, a long breath held between presence and absence, exile and homecoming, injustice and irretrievable loss.

Voices in the Current

Poems of power, place, and systems that exclude. These pieces speak truth into public wounds and name what the world would rather forget.

Mistakes

They say mistakes aren't stumbling blocks,
but stepping stones to success.
Who reap these benefits? I protest.
Is it the privileged, hoarding life's treasure chests,
or the poor, burdened and in distress?
Woe to the piety that forgets the oppressed.
For, believe it or not, the story isn't finished yet.
Into this mix, religion casts its age-old net;
people grappling for power, irreverent and cold.
Steeped in their vices, attitudes their God abhorred.
The flocks remain in distress, the Gospel untold,
leaving me restless, uneasy, and questions unexplored.

Years have passed, and my naïveté lies dead.
Each error pulls life's quilt by its thread.
I've been ensnared, wounded, and tested by sin,
I escaped death by chance, or was it Allah?
"Am I cursed?" you ask, with a twisted sense of humor.
"Oh, come on, no threat," I sighed beneath my breath.
I'm not cursed; I'm a traveler on the sure path to death.
I've made countless mistakes, a fact so stark,
yet the promised success seems lost in the dark.
Mistakes were my tutors in life's ruthless tests,
giving lessons first and assessments next.

In the twilight of my years, I reflect, I ponder:
do the fruits of our errors grant equal power?
A new night, new missteps, and a chilling truth
echo in my chambers where regrets reside.
Even my flaws are sculpted into beauty,
confronting the heart that dismissed the sun
because it had secrets to hide.

No Place

No place was found for them.
From whence you came, how long have you been here?
These questions hang in the air.
Despite our divergent genesis through time's passage,
we share a common ancestry.
Some journeyed through the Middle Passage,
the heart of West and Central Africa.
Some came against their will, some reversed colonization.
For their loved ones, they sought to build an empire.

The wind rushes on, carrying a trail of stolen lives,
laden with cries from distant shores.
Standing on docks, gales howling like a dirge,
they thought not of their progeny,
now stripped of their roots,
an outrage eclipsing even the scandal of the Cross.
For guests in transit, they were.
While some find a fit, for many, there is no place.
This speaks to an inability to adapt,
a fear to embrace something different, or perhaps
a place and people who refuse to know or understand.

This resonates with the displaced in society,
highlighting bigotry fueled by the power of privilege.
Is there no place for ethnic minorities?
Are we excluded, and you, the sole benefactor
of an invisible social system?

I thought it could not get worse,
but poverty, stinging like salt on a wound,
summons tears that once refused to flow,
intensified by threads of deconstruction.

This thread is a creed etched deep in society's soul,
upholding a fractured vision of being—
shaping our collective reality and exposing a world
that smothers opposing views beneath conformity's weight.
In this awakened world, my skin is a target for cruelty,
my liberties fade under statutes disguised as progress.
Open hostility towards women remains immutable,
leaving me to navigate a silence that screams for change.
Modifications in form and appearance offer little relief,
and unchanged DNA sparks outrage over nuanced identity
fueling enduring discrimination against women.

Is it their Blackness, or is there simply no place for them?
 We are marked by sexism,
  wounded by heterosexism,
   and shaped by patriarchism.
We are restrained by ableism,
 contradicted by feminism,
  and rejected by the tendrils of racism.
We are enticed by consumerism,
 polarized by the fervor of wokeism,
  left bewildered in a maze of modern rhetoric.

This ennead wrestles for power,
seeking supremacy across all institutions:
religion, politics, mass media, and law.
Their policies and practices interface,
supporting a narrow view of "normal,"
removing all that does not fit.
The pain is immense, as tears go unnoticed.
The quest for acceptance is now akin
to ghosts wandering in neglected catacombs,
the hope for belonging lies buried,
a relic of time's boundless tomb.

Love as Infrastructure

We often reduce love to a feeling: romantic, familial,
or spiritual. But in reality, love functions as
infrastructure, the architecture that supports identity,
power, politics, legacy, faith, and well-being. When
that infrastructure is nourished, people thrive. When
it's denied or distorted, whole systems collapse.

We become through the love we're given;
the soul's first kindling and its undoing.
But I have seen it shape a frame,
the scaffold of a nation's dreaming.
It bears the weight of what we build,
it steadies breath and anchors will.
Yet when it fails or goes unfilled,
the air itself can turn and kill.

Love shapes power, politics, perception.
A nation speaks as if it knows you,
yet cannot hold your face with care.
It offers law, but not acclaim,
and leaves your hopes exposed to air.
It coils in ribs, it sears the skin,
a hunger born from old desire
to be received, and held within.

We build monuments to quiet the ache.
For not all dominion springs from pride,
but from the grief that went uncried.
It takes up arms and swells the tide.
Unloved, the heart may seek control,
and clothe its hurt in flags and cries.
For power flows from a longing soul
that builds empires from what it craves.

What breaks us is not the weight itself.
We carve our conduct from our lack,
and crown our wounds with sacred goals.
What we resist still shapes the soul.
Resistance may wear a mask,
and trauma preserved is grief in stone.
The self once held will cease to ask;
the self denied must build alone.

The hallowed wears the shape of home.
The heart's first shelter frames the holy.
We kneel where once we feared to lose,
and serve the voice we never praised.
A faith shaped by a parent's glance
may bind the spirit to a cage.
Love turned to test or grim romance
can sanctify unspoken rage.

Systems tremble when love is denied,
while marble walls suppress the sound
of hunger dressed in grand display,
and solitude thrives though wealth abounds.
A nation built on cold commands
will crumble, though its laws remain.
What isn't held by human hands
cannot be ruled by gold or name.

Things fall apart when love's not nurtured.
The church may split over what it claims,
and nations crack when lives ignored.
But absence wears a thousand names,
and coldness cuts where words are stored.
A wound dismissed becomes a law;
where love is not, the roots will gnaw,
and systems starve for what they need.

Let new foundations tend the wound.
Don't look for fault in roof or beam,
dig beneath what love hadn't made,
and name the loss that haunts the dream.
Rebuild with truth, not borrowed praise;
Plant dignity where pain once lived.
For even ash can form new days,
and strength returns where love forgives.

Rainbow

Diamond tears fracture the white sunlit sky,
splintering the rain's tranquil, bluish haze.
A rainbow arcs over this dreary, dour land,
its other end fading into a murky expanse.
No need for Indigo's wisdom to see
the folly in chasing a mythical pot of gold.
Is seven minutes, months, or millennia enough
to grasp the elusive promises of the lofty rainbow?

The only covenant I discern between you and me
lies in the magnetic pull of hidden affections,
in how you infuse my life with vibrant hues.
Yet, my love, cloaked in the shroud of clouds,
burns red with passion, a furnace within,
and dances orange with concealed joy..
When the twin stars of jealousy tinge me yellow,
and envy paints me a malevolent green,
you, draped in a robe of regal violet,
unsettle my soul, and I lose my poise.

Seven pleas to the heavens, seeking your grace.
Love, born in the vivid iridescent arc,
shatters with the sun's wine-black eclipse.
Yet, within the spectrum of emotions dwells
a tale of darker shades left unsaid,
where lust and loneliness endlessly wrestle,
and my desire surges like torrid-carmine tides.

Wrestling with the Alphas

Like wolves, we roam the rugged hills of existence,
traversing tundras and dense, verdant forests.
The fractured black sky looms over our haven,
while I lag behind the pack, steeped in solitude.
Our Alphas, the stars, pierce the shifting dark,
guiding our hunt with their vigilant watch,
their challenge is silent yet ever-present.

Prey is always near, arousing my primal senses.
Yet it's freedom I pursue with measured steps;
a dance with destiny beneath fate's watchful eyes.
It is not the kill nor the savage grip I seek,
I hunger for the nourishment to sustain my restless spirit,
while tested and tempered by the Alphas' scrutiny.

And then there's the moon, at which I howl.
A cry of defiance against its celestial pull,
echoing my battle with other cosmic overseers.
The Alphas provoke my soul, ferocious and fierce,
urging me to cease my rebellion with destiny,
to rise and claim my role as leader of the pack.

Yet I roam with the others, a sightless brood,
tottering, striving to discern the world we inhabit.
The stars guide us, yet leave us yearning.
Each step a question, unanswered in the tundra,
creating meaning from illusion in this endless night,
a paradox of motion tethered to despair.

Others from the litter vie with me;
rivalry spirals through every twitch and glance.
They thought of me as the runt,
paces too measured, a spirit too strange.
Their fangs glint with ritual contempt,
but I carry the weight of survival in my marrow,
and a hunger that outpaces their threats.

As the rogue in our pack, I seize every chance
to stake my claim in scents the wild obeys,
a revolt against the tracks laid by the Alphas.
Wherever I roam, I assert my right to belong,
defying imposed scripts to write my own story.

In destiny's grip, beneath the Alphas' gaze,
I find resolve to challenge their authority.
I carve my path in starlight and moonbeams,
no longer merely a follower in the shadows,
but a wanderer enlightened, charting a course
where every step is mine, guided yet free.

A Piece of Pie, Please

In the heart of our town, in the public square,
we crave a piece of pie and dream of tomorrows.
We stand, bold, though burdened by despair,
for even the darkest days cast their shadows.

In halls, theaters, and café spots,
from bustling streets to the digital sphere;
on social threads where debates run hot,
in every square, our voices are clear.

Visible, like the midday sun;
shining for all, across life's passage.
In diverse tongues, we speak as one,
welcoming all, no matter their language.

Intentional, like the lighthouse's beam,
far-reaching, steadfast, guiding the throng.
In righting wrongs, we build a team;
our every word and deed proves we belong.

"A piece of pie, please" is our humble cry
in every land where countless voices blend.
Our hearts beat in pride for dreams daring to fly
and a vision shared for freedom that won't end.

Yet, in the shadows, faces linger unseen,
barred from the table, their fates unknown,
denied a slice for reasons so mean:
citizenship, borders, lines drawn to disown.

In hushed tones and hands reaching for hope,
"A piece of pie, please," though not free to be.
In foreign lands, they cope incognito,
fearing the notice that will end their spree.

Their stories are woven with threads of pain,
dreaming of a pie they cannot openly share.
In silence, they languish, their hope in vain,
while the world grows too distant to care.

Let's heed the sighs in the heart of the city,
moaning beneath oppression's sting.
Dreaming of freedom beyond self-pity.
For them, this pie means everything.

Clear and bold as an artist's keystrokes,
the plea, "A piece of pie," resounds not in vain.
It calls not for sameness but to shatter the yokes;
seeking equity, free from disdain.

In our call for a piece of pie,
we illuminate paths to love's universal rule.
Our right to the communal feast they must not deny.
Intentional in every step, design, and tool.

In these words, rhymes, and our collective dream,
we rise as one through the changing seasons.
In city squares, under the sky's broad beam,
we stand united, grounded in reason.

We form a quilt of humanity's experience,
rich and diverse across genders and orientations.
In all squares, we claim our rightful existence,
claiming our slice of pie, our shared aspirations.

Free

I choose to leave my home, if only for a time,
to explore life and my constrained desires,
to taste the thrill of a first kiss.
I pack light—small items
that carry immeasurable weight:
a photo album, a collage of boyhood friends,
memories, and emotions held in my heart.
I survey my home one last time
and inhale sharply, drawing courage
from the thought of freedom.

Parting is herculean, draining,
requiring strength beyond this world.
My mother's eyes glisten with unshed tears,
my sister walks with me, a companion
for this final stretch.
My brothers stand stoic, their tears veiled,
avoiding any public show of affection.
These moments, taut with emotion,
nearly sway me to stay.
Yet the journey awaits. I must obey.

The road and destiny call. I must answer.
Through a city of webs, along a river of asphalt,
I pass new roads stretching into the unfamiliar.
From the cab's window, the world passes by:
crowded cityscapes yield to open roads,
single lanes, trailing pastures, and docks.
A mosaic of humanity of all shades, shapes,
and sizes recedes into the distance.

As each familiar landmark fades,
the vehicle draws nearer to an uncharted future.
The sweet allure of self-realization beckons,
freedom to explore well-hidden urges.
Gazing through the window, landscapes blur;
a smile breaks on my face,
a fleeting taste of freedom.
For now, at least, I am truly free,
blind to the fate that lies ahead.

Seduced and Bitten

I stopped for a drink at a club rumored to fulfill every fantasy.
It was a place where everyone mingled,
the marginalized and the privileged,
those who sampled the local fleshly male
or female fare alongside their heterosexual partners.
I perched at the bar, a drink in hand,
reluctant to scan the room and risk recognition.
I felt foolish in this dark room of anonymity;
even had I wished to survey the crowd,
the dimmed lights cloaked everyone in obscurity.

From the shadows, a figure approached;
their perfume ignited my senses.
A voice, smoky and mellowed by maturity, whispered,
"Hi, darling, do you need company?"
My heart fluttered with excitement and apprehension,
as the possibility of pleasure presented itself.
I was offered another drink and accepted.
The words, "You are a beauty; heaven must have sent you,"
sent shivers, a sweet torment, down my spine.
I blushed, laughed,
and unwittingly made my first mistake.

I awoke to the city's distant hum.
"Strange," I thought, "this isn't my usual rowdy hotel."
Slowly, consciousness crept in.
My breath was laden with the stench of alcohol.
I wondered where I was.
The pain in my lower extremities
made it difficult to breathe.
My intimate parts pulsated
with an unspeakable ache, and I felt feverish inside.

with an unspeakable throbbing; my skull ached
and my stomach churned in agony.
Even the slightest gesture jolted
my aching body to its core,
its desperate plea for relief unheeded.
Memories began to surface:
being overpowered, invaded.
Suddenly, my eyes flew open.
I tried to rise but failed,
my limbs too weak to obey.
Thoughts of being held down
and violated again flooded my mind.

Fueled by defiance, I forced myself up,
my eyes adjusting to the consuming darkness.
Like Adam and Eve deceived by a serpent's charm,
I stood exposed, ashamed, and exploited.
I searched for a place to clean myself up,
longing to wash away the night's dishonor.
But I quickly realized such cleansing
would erase the traces of the horrific event.
With sluggish movements, I hunted for my clothes.
I found them reeking of liquor, sweat, and blood.
I reached for the door, inhaled deeply,
and stepped outside.
I shuffled forward, unsure of my destination.
I only knew I had to escape.
I wobbled on, feeling sullied.
The sight of a familiar police post brought relief
and a sense of dread.

Political Débâcles
aka Jackass Seh Di Wurl Nuh Level

Lawd, mi belly battam a hat mi!
Mi caan fiin nuh wud fi diskribe dis debaacle,
but jackass did seh di wurl nuh level.

Caught in the tumult of political rumpuses.
The city and Congress were held hostage.
These debacles, bidden, trumped all logic,
thrusting the Capitol into a chilling frenzy.
Escape from this barrage, the perpetual chatter,
the fiasco rippling across online platforms
and traditional media was futile.

There was nowhere to run, nowhere to hide.
Being unwilling spectators, we absorbed it all.
We longed for peace, a moment to pray,
to ponder the fate our kin now face,
to un-taste the bitterness of tainted tidings,
Tantrums unfurled like storm clouds,
darkening the fragile horizon of hope.

We listened, we watched, and what we saw
was a nation divided; hearts laden with despair.
In anguish, some shaved their heads in disbelief,
families fractured, and friendships abandoned.
Arrogance and superiority are wielded as blades;
with every gnashing of teeth and cries of dismay,
the land teetered closer to utter disarray.

A chameleon's pledge, bold and obscure,
while Hill Myna mocked a world drenched in red.
The Barque sailed on, steady and poised.
Is it that fox who set the fields ablaze?
Or was the fire always there, waiting to rise;
a nation in its stark, sobering reckoning,
exposed for the world's eyes to see.

Plagued by protests, mutiny, and police abuse,
amid bold cries against inequality.
Are we still in the throes of a pandemic?
And what of the claims of a resurgence
of White supremacy?

An armed populace advanced across the lawn,
breaching the Chamber with defiant steps.
An alternate debate raged within my mind,
a stark contrast to the True North's realities.
Do plants destroy their seedlings before they bloom,
or is the harvest still sacred, even when cut too soon?
As consent sinks low do we await the scandalous rise
of an Elagabalus under indifferent skies?
Still, they trudge on, unmoved by the people's cries?

Black voices demanded their right to life
unarmed advocates of nonviolence,
met with vicious force by a system
sworn to protect them.
Had they been the ones storming the Capitol,
the carnage would have been unspeakable,
a sight that would make the world recoil in horror.
But justice is not vengeance,
and pain must not invert into power plays.
In a world increasingly polarized by race,
White voices now fear erasure more than dominance.

This, too, is a symptom of how deeply broken we are.
For across the old empires that once preached liberty,
freedom falters at the stake of polite furor.
Women vanish beneath well-meaning banners,
and tongues are bound by law, not by terror.
Those who harm conceal it behind virtue,
while those who question are swallowed by shame.
Solidarity is replaced by suspicion,
and history, in a few elite hands, is reshaped as revenge.

We cannot heal by reversing the wound;
pain multiplied does not yield peace.
White children should not inherit guilt,
nor Black children the arrogance of revenge.
We seek a world where memory teaches,
not where it avenges.

History, preserved within her sacred pages,
traces of anger's winds fanning reckless blazes.
To target one community to address chaos
is akin to burning the barn to kill a few rats.

Lawd, mi belly battam a hat mi!
Mi caan fiin nuh wud fi diskribe dis debaacle,
but jackass did seh di wurl nuh level.

Quid Pro Quo

A bribe misconstrues ethical standards and fair play,
provoking and taunting in its resilient display.
Is this the stench of disdain, the undertow of hate,
or a web woven with vexation, disorder's bait?

We grasp for love but seize hate's jagged bars,
while ancestral spirits, like distant stars,
cast glimmers of hope through mazes of scars,
clearing the soul's illusions, dissolving discrimination,
unraveling divisions shaped by unjust provisions.

Perpetual racial profiling heightens fear and tension,
a familiar trend with parallels too numerous to mention.
A narrative of overrepresentation and social intervention
aligns with programs of worrying intention,
beckoning a fractured future for our descendants,
as they weigh the worth of all that was given,
against the cost of what was taken.

Treaties rewrote history, yet our ancestors bore the blame
for relinquishing rights, promises made in good faith,
solemn vows to lay the foundations for generations to come,
to secure a future, though the melody of finance hums.
Lump sums, annual restitution in history's narration;
an unintended prelude to unwelcome assimilation,
a fate, they argued, that was never the intention.

Monkey Business

In this fractured world we inhabit,
sociopolitical machinations dominate.
The privileged feast on the underprivileged,
idolizing power and possessions,
elevating nations and nature to divine statuses.
Such landscapes, overseen by narcissists,
are devoid of any shred of empathy.
A nation, stage-managed, a carefully cultivated image,
spinning a myth to mask its true colors: a perception
concealing the absence of political accountability.

Behind the doors of governance lies another force,
corporate lobbyists wielding their golden strings.
Interest groups with millions buy their way,
shaping policies to fit their profit margin.
The people's will, drowned in seas of greed
where corporations write laws the rest must heed.
The average citizen's search for truth
is met with silence, redacted, delayed,
or outright denied.

Contempt and disdain are proudly worn like badges,
while self-love and arrogance thrive unchecked.
Rejection of this pomp and vanity
is defiance against the tyranny of false grandeur.
This marked a national brush with catastrophe;
mobs, long fueled and stirred by revered leaders,
more concerned with their glory than our poverty.
They exhibited greed and folly, the traits of fanatics.
Mark but this! Where laws are hostile, dissent takes root.

A grim day unfolded in our cities and streets;
our forebears would scoff and call it "monkey business."
The old saying rings true: "Monkey see, monkey do."
Rioters swung from balconies and scaled walls like beasts.
Enforcers and rebels engaged in a fierce tug-of-war,
a grotesque game, barriers swinging to a grim rhythm.
It was a spectacle, charged with jolts of adrenaline
and fear, casting ripples of chaos, captivating and somber,
a theater where the thrill and terror of the actors
buzzed in the ears and flashed before the eyes
of besieged spectators.

In the melee, House members scrambled in desperation
for makeshift covers. The barbarism that unfolded!
    Anarchy and arrogance,
        bigotry and brutality,
            cronyism and corruption,
                deceit and destruction.
                    Such insidious insolence
                      shamelessly sashaying
                        through the session.

Blood-stained walls laden with graffiti,
tear gas, extinguishers, shattered glass, and banners;
debris forming a macabre obstacle course,
eclipsing the squalor of any refuse site.
It revealed a systemic issue:
the scorn cast at those crossing borders,
a disdain for the marginalized and outsiders.
Even the settler majority bore wounds,
criticized for daring to claim their right to vote.
In towering jungles of concrete and steel,
the voices of historical minorities rise,
favoring indigo's vigor over ochre's valor.

The rioters' garb, eccentric and grotesque,
formed a parade of pandemonium.
Their garments mirrored the Joker's sinister pride,
a carnival of madness and buffoonery,
as if plucked from Gotham's most notorious scene.
Draped in vibrant hues, each rioter was a canvas
of rebellion and defiance,
adorned with the remains of beasts,
a sight to inflame an activist's blood,
boiling over into a cauldron of protest and rally.
Prepared for battle, they stood clad in protective gear,
shields raised for any impending assault,
aggressive and belligerent in their fortified stance.

In the aftermath, arrests trickled like shallow streams.
Yet eye-opening in their revelation.
The loss of life is a lamentable tragedy;
even one death is one too many.
Yet, this chaos unearthed a grave injustice
preferential treatment based on a person's skin color.
In the madness, I wondered who the real witch was
to be condemned to face the gallows?
This debacle lays bare the sickness
in a system crying out for reform.
A stark reminder that if the foundation is weak,
mere platitudes are futile and won't do any good.
We deluded ourselves, believing a fool to be a savior,
a grievous miscalculation, embarking on a fool's errand,
entangled in a web of confusion and delusion, caught in
the chaos of whether this "monkey business"
was a calculated plot or an insidious agenda.

A Rare Invention

Alas! I am bound by a perplexing dilemma,
my soul wrestling with a daunting revelation,
the unsettling thought: I am naught but dust.
To unravel this enigma, I turned to ancient scriptures,
seeking to grasp the essence of my existence.
Within their pages lies a claim of great weight:
we are divinely created, fashioned for eternity,
ignited with the potential to shape reality.

Humanity was entrusted with naming all creatures,
but does this confer dominion over all creation?
To see in each being its intrinsic nature,
to answer the call of fruitfulness without greed,
to cultivate presence while planting *seeds*,
to harness with compassion the essence of the Earth,
and honor the integrity of its cardinal design.

Can this task vanish beneath the sunlight of progress?
This majestic framework preserves the spirit of our rights.
Then why do we fear the loss of what was never ours?
From the allure of invention, the future takes root.
While legends say humanity is formed from stardust,
others believe we arose from the Earth's crust,
beings of rarity, we breathe the breath of life.

We stand as conduits through which Life radiates.
Be awestruck by this beauty, let your spirit soar.
But bear in mind this breathtaking truth:
in our veins churns the current of a rare invention.

Not My Story

No single ideology can speak for all humanity.
Each vision of the good and right bears its flaws,
its eccentricities crafting the framework of policies.
You forced your values upon us,
and when we rejected them, hostility reigned,
fracturing bonds, severing territories,
as the peddler of hegemony claimed victory.
You sought to mold us in your likeness,
creating an irreversible shift,
and this, in one direction only.

"It's mandatory!"
Boarding schools became tools of assimilation,
forcing our people into your traditions, your structure.
But what of our philosophy?
The sacredness of all living things,
the law of nature, mutual support.
Still, you say, "I had no part in it.
It's a part of history, not my story."

Liberalism and Capitalism, judged the fairest ideologies,
imposed their ethos and paradigms upon nations,
yet were the cruelest of all unholy inventions.
I can speak for my African ancestry, but not for others,
those who faced annihilation through countless wars
and acts of deculturation.
This—not only by one colonial administration.
These experiences left us fractured.
Yet, you say, "I had no part in it.
It's a part of history, not my story."

Alas! The tragedy of this situation:
our offspring subjected to constant criminalization,
their actions shaped by unprocessed trauma,
the lingering effects of forced occupation.
Again, you say, "I had no part in it,
it's a part of history, not *my* story."

You are the inheritor of your ancestors' wealth.
Where do you think they got it from?
Spare us your pity and deceptive kindness.
Grant us the power for self-governance,
return the land you hold to our seventh generation,
and allow us the liberty to live our way of life.
Yes, it is also your story.
You are the inheritor of history and our shared legacy.

Don't dismiss the past as distant and done.
History speaks in the walls you build
and the hands holding what others have lost.
Will you heed the demands of justice
or silence them beneath the weight of denial?
This story is ours to share,
it's inseparable pain and its possibilities,
a reckoning and a chance to begin again.

Turning Tables

We are the foundation upon which this nation stands,
the embodiment of its human rights and mores.
Power was withheld from the oppressed and voiceless,
while history chains the curious and crowns the complicit.
We voice our remorse for wounds once inflicted,
for our role in fostering the vestiges of xenophobia,
the hunger for conquest, the scars of forced migrations.
Deep marks remain, each one heavy with regret,
and the lines, once drawn, remain unbroken.
What's mine is mine, and it won't be taken.

Can we be absolved of our ancestors' sins?
You were "other" in their eyes. They were alien in yours.
Were their actions driven by fear of losing power,
a panicked response to that first encounter?
They were reckless, erratic, and bound by fragile pride.
Has the pendulum of life swung wide,
shifting the view from your side to mine?
In these questions, the seeds of revolution lie.

Through the cracks of time, the past bleeds its tragedies.
Is history's wheel circling back to where it began:
us becoming you, and you, like our past selves?
Do not claim this land for those yet to be born,
as penance for sins of forebears long gone.
Does justice demand complete reparation
from those now distant from the first generation,
who peered through mirrors of fears
and wanting to be kind, were cruel instead?

Will forgiveness sprout where guilt takes root,
or do seeds of sorrow yield only thorns?
If tables turn, will we grasp the weight of their burden
or simply build new walls, reversing the chains?
Can we dismantle what was forged in the fires of greed
to rebuild, not from ashes, but from resilience,
empathy, and human dignity?

Decorum or Desire

Double-dipping fried ravioli in cheesy marinara sauce
is far better than going from one hole to another.
Still, the fruit of knowledge ripens in every age.
Golf is a precision club-and-ball sport,
where players compete, wielding an array of clubs,
aiming to strike balls into waiting holes
with as few strokes as possible.

Each course is a challenge, each stroke a pursuit.
It takes time to get there, but that's the aim.
Economics, much like marinara sauce, blends essentials,
scrutinizing the production and allocation of goods
and services, all dependent on a fragile honor system.
The wheel turns, yet freedom always demands its price:
to hit is to miss, and to miss is to strike again.

Do I fear losing what was never mine to hold?
An honor system, both frail and fierce in its demand,
is sustained by trust,
but without enforcing the rules regulating its code,
is no different than moving from hole to hole,
or dipping a crisp twice into the same sauce.
Frowns can't be helped after nibbling a crisp,
then re-dipping it.
It's like taking twice from the same basket,
reaping double doles where one was due.

It doesn't matter whether hands, feet,
nose, or some other appendage are involved.
If any find themselves on their knees,
I'm uncertain whether to cheer or jeer.
With this, many will disagree…
Ahem. Or perhaps… agree.

Like Spiders

Our behavior is fascinating, evolutionary to a fault.
Quietly, we lie in wait, predators in the open,
luring the unsuspecting into intricate snares of deceit,
ensnaring them in our shackles; silken and perilous.

Faced with danger, our actions defy logic:
a masquerade, a pretense of oblivion.
We feign lifelessness, a deceptive hoax.
Like spiders, masters of entrapment,
we morph into instruments of conquest.

Webs, spun from silks of ambition, form our fortresses,
sanctuaries where we brood, unwittingly wasted.
Displays of aggression, a spectacle of force;
fuel battles for sex, power, dominion, and supremacy.

Our pursuits are driven by insatiable hunger:
wealth, carnal desires, the intoxicating pull of status.
In this chase, friendship and love are casualties,
relegated to afterthoughts in our grander schemes.

Numbness creeps in—a cold, callous indifference
to the wreckage spun in our pursuit of destiny.
Ensnared by the traps we create for others,
we are architects of our ruin,
spinning, spinning, lost in a poisonous
labyrinth of our own making.

Scars That Speak

Here, longing becomes language. These poems reveal how grief, rejection, and fractured love leave scars—scars that still remember how to speak.

In Two Worlds, I Grieve

Part 1: Arrival at the Graveside

I arrive at the graveyard to sunlight filters through the trees,
stitched threads, carefree and wedded to the breeze.
Daylight's hand shapes my dreams into jagged nightmares.
In searching for your tombstone, I see how each shrub
stands sentinel, each blade of grass a living monument to Us.
This routine has become my world, my normal, everyday life,
a quiet conversation with the past.

I seek your name amid these living memorials:
moss-kissed stones, ancient yews, a verdant carpet
under which the departed sleep.
Their bodies, long returned to the soil,
nourishing the roots beneath my feet.
Ah. Finally, there you are.

Kneeling, I clear the debris from your grave.
A task that transcends mortal understanding.
It's a duty felt in the soul, expressed through tears,
and carried out with the stoic determination of love and logic.

"Hi, my love, I am here. How are you?"
I speak into the air heavy with the silence of unsaid sentiments,
laden with the weight of time since I last talked to you.
It's summer again, and life at the cottage,
our sanctuary by the lake is alive and abuzz with activity.
Yet without you, the world feels smaller, its pulse slower.

Part II: Your Smile, the Island, the Ache

I think of Jamaica's coasts:
beaches boasting sands of white, brown, and gray,
crystal-clear waters lapping at the shores.
Palm trees swaying in rhythm with the island's heart,
their fronds flirting with the wind,
dipping and twirling to the ocean's lullaby.
Splendid coconuts hanging like nature's jewels,
poised to quench a thirst that lingers deep within.

The sun, ever the ruler of this paradise, parades across
the horizon, painting the sky in cascades of radiant color.
Majestic mountains rise in the distance, their misty peaks
guarding the island's ancient secrets.
Yet in my heart, you, my beloved, surpass these charms.

O, how I long to return, to feel the island's caress once more,
to relive the days when Jamaica was less a place,
and more a dream we lived, where every breath carried
the sea's fragrance and the melody of your laughter.
Your teeth, bright as pearls against ebony skin,
still visit my slumber.
Your smile could illuminate the darkest corners of my soul.

Yet here I am, caught between two worlds, grieving.
Bound by memory to one, the other a distant border.
My heart mourns the absent tide lapping at golden shores
where crimson hibiscus unfurl their joyous petals.
I'm trapped in the North's icy grip
where sorrow carves its lines upon my brow
and the wind howls like caged beasts.

I pause, fingers trailing over the cold, carved stone,
feeling the weight of time etched in every groove;
a wordless exchange with what remains.
Each letter whispers of a life once lived.
Your name, now a chapter closed,
bears the bittersweet taste of lamentation,
a beauty found only in the chalice of loss.

I keep vigil in the hush between us,
wrapping my thoughts around you.
The silence doesn't last long. It never does.
I have much to say,
for in your presence, my soul finds its tongue.

Part III: *The Birds Remember*

Yesterday, I watched the eagles, their wings wide,
soaring high, slicing through the sky with cries
that cut the silence. The ospreys, your beloved ospreys,
circled endlessly, hovering above the lake, eyes sharp as arrows,
scanning the surface like sentinels of the life we once knew.
Lucy, our lone blue heron, still stalks the shallows,
her graceful silhouette etched against the sunset;
a poignant reminder of you.

The cawing of a murder of crows pulls me from my soliloquy;
ink-black darts carving their path through the air.
How ironic that they gather here,
mocking my beloved's unsolved murder.
Their cries echo the grief lodged in my heart,
a mournful dirge that will not fade.
Each black feather a shadowy reminder
of the darkness that has settled in.

With their relentless cawing, these crows remind me
of the times we sat on the balcony, watching them by the lake.
Last Thursday, their squawks filled the empty spaces,
their rattling "caw-caw-caw" cutting through the stillness,
as if to fend off the quiet that has lingered since you left.

The ravens, darker and larger, loom ever-present.
Their deep-throated "kraa, kraa, kraa"
reverberates in the distance.
Their shadows stretch long, creeping across the lawn,
a constant reminder of the void you've left behind.
Their presence looms heavily, like your love,
casting shadows across the fading light of my days.

I saw the kingfisher the other day,
hovering like a suspended thought,
then plunging into the lake,
briefly rupturing the water's glassy face.
It mirrored my heart's descent into the depths
of loneliness, where waves of grief pull me under,
leaving me gasping for breath.

You would love the cacophonous chorus of seagulls,
their "kyow, kyow" mingled with sharp "kree-ar."
At times, a gang gathers, their calls rapid and insistent,
blending with a mocking "ha-ha-ha" bouncing on the water.

I'm still captivated by their antics,
especially the guttural "gwak-gwak" as they squabble
over scraps, their chatter like distant puppies barking.
You would have laughed at how I bolted through the small door,
hitting my head in my haste, convinced the dogs were loose.
Softer cries of "cree-cree" linger, adding an odd dissonance
to the symphony above the lake,
a living chorus of nature's design.

Even the gannets joined, refusing to be left out,
piercing the air with sharp "kah-kahs."
Their strange duet, a call and response,
forms a weird partnership in the sky,
their arcs and dips reflecting your laughter.
It rose and fell with the tides, a melody
that lingers long after the sound has faded.

Part IV: Not Buried, but Carried

Exhausted from recounting the birds' behaviors to my beloved,
I move to the foot of the grave, brushing the earth
with my fingers, pulling stubborn weeds from the ground,
pausing to recover my labored breath.

Tidying your resting place, a small act of care,
feels woefully insufficient. Silence settles around me,
its weight pressing heavy with the loss I bear.
Each breath reminds me of the void that now fills my days.

I clear away fallen leaves, remnants of seasons past,
wishing I could do more; wishing I could bring you back.
If only for a moment, to share this tender ritual of love.

Ah, darling, I must tell you of the squirrels who visited often.
Their antics paled in comparison to the raccoons;
those masked marauders who raided the bird feeder
and drank their fill without a second thought.

You would have rebuked me, your kind spirit
always finding joy in protecting nature's quirks.
But oh well, I have to share this with you:
I smeared the metal post with coconut oil
to thwart their nightly looting.
It was a wickedly funny sight,
those relentless bandits slipping and sliding,
like clowns on ice, paws scrambling in vain,
still unwilling to give up the hunt.

Their frustrated faces, so full of mischief and resolve,
made me laugh aloud, despite myself.
Even with my heart aching for you, in that moment,
I felt you with me, your laughter mingling with mine,
as it always did, turning even the smallest joy
into something sacred.

On sunny days, I'd sit for hours on the deck,
watching as kayaks traced ripples, their trails
like ink lines drawn across a living canvas.
Canoes glided quietly, and pontoon boats drifted lazily,
carrying streams of laughter that felt so familiar.
Paddleboarders carved wavy paths through the waters,
each vessel stirring memories that refused to fade.
It was as if the lake itself remembered us,
its currents churning with living echoes,
holding onto you as I do

But lately, this serene scene has been interrupted.
Jet skis and speedboats tearing through at reckless speeds,
their noise startling me, the geese, and all nearby.
Still, I found unexpected joy in watching the red
and white maple-leafed flags flutter at the boats' sterns,
daring the wind to test its resolve.
Ah, such lovely sights and sounds,
yet missing from them all was the scent and touch of you.

Meals haven't been the same without you.
Thanks to a good friend, *Jabbar*, I sampled
authentic codfish and beans.
I must admit, my attempt to replicate it was a disaster;
too much burned sugar and half-cooked beans.
What I ended up with was a dull, disappointing dish.
But her strawberry shortcake was a sweet joy;
a slice of heaven itself.
I brought a few pieces with me to share with you,
though you always said no one's desserts
could ever match the ones we made together.
I still remember the mess we made in the kitchen;
flour in your hair, mischief in your eyes.
Nothing tastes the same without you.

The scent of coffee in the morning air now carries a pang,
a bittersweet reminder of the mornings we shared,
when your laughter mingled with the rich aroma,
filling the kitchen with a warmth I can't seem to recreate.
Yet I carry what cannot be buried.

Part V: Until Next Time

I pause for a moment, then sit again by the grave.
Gazing toward the heavens, I see the sun dipping low,
casting long shadows across the earth as if even
the day itself understands it's time to say goodbye.

I linger a while longer, resting my hand on the headstone,
feeling the cool, unyielding surface beneath my fingertips.
A final, silent connection before I must leave.
Bowing my head, forehead pressed to the tombstone,
I breathe through my tears, whispering,
"Until we meet again, my love.
May your soul find peace in this quiet place,
far from the turbulence of the harbor that took you,
and the hands that led you there."

These words are not a farewell but a promise.
Until next time.
With a heavy heart, I turn and leave, carrying with me
the echoes of your memory.
I hope that somehow, you hear me in the wind,
feel me in the warmth of the sun on the earth that cradles you.

The birds still sing their songs, the lake still laps at the shore.
In every breath of wind, every ripple on the lake,
I am touched by you, Da'Vinovah.
Gone from this world, but this place,
like my heart, will always hold you close.

The Touch That Spoke

You heard "I love you," yes, a hundred times,
yet it was the closeness that changed the frame.
The words were like wind, the warmth a chime,
that touch spoke language words dare not name.

If I had stilled the arms that sought to hold,
and left unspoken the gesture of my heart,
would love oft spoken make your world unfold,
or be lost without the touch that sets it apart?

Perhaps the weight of longing left in voice
could not map the contours of my ache.
The hug revealed love's natural choice,
a silent oath I never meant to break.

If I had held back, would more remain?
Or was that moment all I had to gain?

The Moon Within My Scar

In my soul, a habitat of crystalline blues,
the moon ascends, not from the sky alone,
but birthed from mirrored depths below,
a frozen sea cradling its misty sorrow.

A solitary creature lingers, still as the dawn,
trapped in the fracture of time and glass.
Shards of longing scatter like broken dreams,
their glow a hymn to what cannot last.

Like a wolf, I wear defiance as my pelt.
Eyes like embers, feral, fierce.
The night rages at me, a murder of crows in tow,
echoing the desires that tether me.

This inner world, both desolate and divine,
is a battlefield where lovers confide.
Here, longing collides with the infinite
and souls nurse their fractures, their sacred scars.

Negative

I sat in my family's home,
enveloped in a shroud of hopelessness.
Helpless in the silence,
I grappled with a looming fate,
questioning my past actions,
lamenting the choices I'd made.
Had I been more cautious, more reserved,
abstaining until love had truly blossomed,
instead of surrendering to fleeting pleasure;
this nightmare might not have befallen me.

The violation was a brutal assault;
a sinister breach of my body's sanctity.
A dark destroyer, a predator of exploitation,
lurking until it could devour my youth;
my naïveté, my untouched innocence.
"Life is so unfair!" I cried inwardly.
From that moment of terror,
my life stalled, frozen in time.

I was lost in thought
until time dragged me forward,
toward the moment of verdict.
The hours crawled, heavy with dread,
each breath thick with anticipation.
In the waiting room, my heart pounded.
A clerk approached, files in tow,
and placed them in the hands of waiting nurses,
who bowed their heads in consultation.

I strained to hear,
but the noise in my head was louder
than the world around me.
An eternity passed before they approached.
"Do they bring bad tidings?" I wondered.
They spoke at last, "Your results have come."
I braced, numbed, expecting the worst.
"Mr. Kay," they echoed my name,
a glimmer of light in their tone,
"Your test was a false positive; you're not infected."

Shock propelled me upright,
an urge to embrace someone, anyone
in this whirlwind of relief.
For a moment, time stood still;
the world held its breath.
Again and again, I checked the results,
inspecting every word, surveying each line,
making sure reality aligned
with what I heard and what I saw.

Tribute to "The Raven" by Edgar Allan Poe

The Golden Shovel poem, "The Unquiet Soul,"
draws inspiration from Edgar Allan Poe's timeless
masterpiece, "The Raven" (1845). Using the
second stanza as its foundation, it crafts a narrative
steeped in the supernatural, echoing Poe's haunting
musicality and despair. Through this intertextual
dance, the dark beauty of Poe's verses is mirrored,
whispering anew to the souls who wander the
liminal spaces of love and loss.

Édouard Manet, The Raven, Library of Congress, Public Domain

The Unquiet Soul

In graveyards of desires, ashen grief hung, and I sighed, "Ah."
Loneliness wrapped me in her cold arms distinctly
marking the hours; I am absorbed in memories. Yet I,
I, lost in November's grip or June's ghost, should remember;
for the chill outside my heart mirrored the chill within it.
The sun dipped, stealing from the sky the beauty it once was.
It stood vulnerable, as bleakness slowly settled in.
While spirits roamed in ruins, untouched by time and the
uninviting calls to a soul seeking salvation from the bleak,
numbing, silent hush, vestiges of the festivities of December.

In the stillness, yearnings climbed like ivy on graves, and
a mournful breeze carried tales from forgotten tombs. Each
from realms where despair and decay refused to separate.
I mourn delights once borne, now dying.
Anguish glinted in my eyes; fears reignited from the ember.
Yet fate's cruel hands poisoned my well of love and wrought
a requiem, draining the joy from my forlorn abode. Its
corridors now void of life, while despairs sown fed the ghost
of my soul. These memories weighed like stones upon
my being, where love's touch had left it cold, like the
fleeting mist beneath my feet on the chilly floor.

Longing for a sign, for warmth once shown, I eagerly
earnestly listened to the past in the creaking, mournful floor. I,
yearning for affection in the silence, all alone, wished.
I wished promises had not faded into the unknown along the
forgotten river. Yet dawn offered no solace. Come the morrow,
in tome after tome, I will seek respite, a quest pursued vainly.
I found no answers in the night's stark monochrome. Yet I
caught a fleeting glimpse of joy, now overthrown, and had
in solitude, where only my thoughts are condoned, sought
vigor from stars that exhaled farewell, flickered, and faded to
seeking security in the moon's ghostly halo. I toiled to borrow.

Scavenged from my soul, a silent scream, a quiet moan from
a heart once a pure place, now a cryptic, heavy throne. My
whispered claims of love, never known. Within the books,
my refuge, places I'd once explored, I found no surcease
from daily battles. My inner gore was merely a remnant of
pain etched upon each page; each line intoned with sorrow.
Each breath, a piercing shard, brought more and more sorrow.
The irony of warmth I never had, for love unborn—for
roars of laughter ringing in my soul no more. So too, the
dreams and traces of kindness no longer bloom, forever lost.
The absence coursing through my veins was not for Lenore.

The rare beauty of his spirit soared, for
magnetic was his laughter, which I did adore. But the
moments of light that briefly shone were rare.
Now, silence speaks louder than folklore, and
his face, obscured by time, shines through, distinctly radiant,
piercing my dreams, like the grace of a maiden
whose soft sighs stir the soul of one utterly lost, to whom
the sorrowful wings of seraphs beckon, and angels
lost in ether beyond our gaze, have no soul to claim, no name
written in the book of love, its pages listing only Lenore.

Yet Vinova dwells in oblivion, in the heart's core, nameless.
Crows' claws cling to dead cedar boughs like scepters here.
Their mocking cries speak of things no soul can atone for.
Still, the cedar over his grave will bloom evermore.

Positive

I lived for the sound of music and the latest trends.
For my parties to be a success,
I attended others' in *round robin*.
My life became a chain of parties,
booze, and sexual pleasures.
Exploration was my creed,
so long as the bills were paid.
I sank into indulgence,
to the point of corruption,
reason slipping away.

Certain ailments force us to play roles,
to feign wellness while friends and foes
scuttle in denial, afraid to name the truth
of my unsightly visage and pending demise.
They whispered, *cancer or tuberculosis.*
Oh, the wise knew. These verdicts were covers.
For long, I had suspected I might be "positive."

When confirmation came,
the words struck harder than a fist;
a sentence to mortality.
Hearing my test was "positive,"
each syllable became a poisoned arrow
and a river of tears flowed from my eyes.
A million daggers pierced my soul,
shards of glass slicing into my spirit.
I became a hollow shell, adrift and shattered.

The sun had kissed my face for less than thirty years,
yet my life was coming to a tragic end.
I wept without restraint,
grief wracking my body violently.
Death approached swiftly.
My complexion darkened,
my skin clung to brittle bones,
bedsores gnawed at my flesh.
Hollow eyes stared from a sinking face.

I don't know which is worse:
this untimely death that feels so unfair,
leaving behind wealth, friends, and fleeting joy,
or facing the world "Positive."

Things Unsaid

Here at my desk, I sit in tears,
gripped by tenebrious, consuming fear.
My co-workers glance, their gazes keen,
startled by my sobs, a daunting scene.

I've never felt such dismal fear in an affair;
a love so fierce it caught me unaware.
Confusion reigns, my emotions askew,
trapped between fearing and loving you.

Haunted by ghosts of my past, among the living, I roam,
where love and hate deny my soul a home.
Among the ruins of dreams, I stumble and long,
a soul unmoored in a world where I don't belong.

When did your spell summon this apocalypse?
Why is my radiance obscured by your eclipse?
I long to be yours, yet loathe the chains that bind,
torn between a caged heart and a resigned mind.

Take off your shades; let me see your eyes,
reveal the truth beneath your disguise.
I long for a melody of trust in your tone,
but insincerity paints the deeds you've shown.

You ask, "What's wrong?" with casual disdain,
and I marvel at your condescending refrain.
I pour out the pain your actions have sown,
the hidden agony, the torments I've known.

You sit and listen, a vacant gaze in your eyes,
inattentive to my anguish, my words, my sighs.
I bare the wounds etched deep within my heart,
and await your response; please, your wisdom impart.

Like shards of glass, your words pierce my soul,
each fragment carving scars that take their toll.
Time slips away like sand from open hands,
some stories are scripted, yet on no pages stand.

Conversations fade, suspended in twilight's yawn.
There are things unsaid, yet in my heart, they spawn.
In these fragile hours, as hope slowly decays,
I sigh in your presence, watching my dream slip away.

A Special Gift

Eleven-year-olds kidnapped,
and families' worlds turned upside down.
Young lives extinguished. Abrupt, senseless, cruel.
Tragedies saw many vanish into murmurs of history.

Through clenched teeth, a parent cries, "This child is mine."
Another whispers, "Here lies my flesh and blood."
Still another: "The fruit of my womb, offspring from my loins."
To me, you were an irreplaceable gift, a star from heaven.
Now, the warmth of my heart has turned cold without you.

Who will share their laughter with me,
offering wisdom beyond their years?
Whose small hand will search for mine
when crossing streets or claiming the TV remote?
Who will fill their pockets with trash as treasures;
innocent spoils of youthful adventures?
Your mischief is the missing piece in our home.

To whom will I teach the complexity of grammar
and the virtues that give life its meaning?
Who will hug me goodbye in the twilight hours
before I rush off to work at night?
Who will be my adventurous companion;
a co-conspirator in innocent schemes?
I cradle your presence, refusing to let it fade,
yet your absence hums in the sorrow I wear.

Who will guide me through their world of movies,
an ambassador of childhood's wonder?
Who will vault from my shoulders at the beach,
a fearless diver chasing the thrill of the waves?
When friends gather to join the fun, who will shout,
"Get your own dad!"?
Your absence echoes in the lullabies I sing.

Yes, I will miss those rosy cheeks and cheeky speech:
"You're going to make a counselor of me."
In you, God gave me His finest treasure,
you were the blessing I never knew I needed.

You are a lasting imprint on the canvas of my mind.
In every quiet moment, in every corner of our home
lies the ghost of your laughter, your unfulfilled dreams.
Each a fragment of a future lost.
Your tiny fingerprints are etched on the walls of my mind,
and in the gallery of my heart, your portrait will hang forever.

The Midas Touch

To touch and be touched, to love and be loved.
The touch of love is life's greatest treasure.
A balm, a soothing hum in a world of noise,
a treasure beyond measure, a source of joy.
But beware the lure of a gilded snare,
whose warmth leaves the heart in despair.
Life is no cartoon, no stories from a book;
it's a canvas painted with nuanced outlooks.
Like King Midas, we can turn hearts to gold,
and wake to find ourselves alone, unloved, and old.

Magnificent and magical time seems well spent,
    with lovers and family, yet the heart's not content.
Intoxication and indulgence are never absolute;
    fame, love, and lust a never-ending pursuit.
Dangers are overlooked, we are blinded by pride,
    submerged in delusions, with nowhere to hide.
Anxious and unsettled as the façade cracks,
    deception's schemes are filled with drawbacks.
Sensual and sophisticated, a sultry game we play;
    beneath the guise of control, gold turns to clay.

In your game of emotions, others become pawns.
Guided by hope, they strive to reclaim what's gone.
A touch that once healed now turns hearts to stone;
a cruel echo of love, leaving pain to atone.
People have hearts; they feel the sting.
Neglect them, abuse them, and they'll return the pain.
Abandoned, bereft of all you've known,
you'll learn the curse of the Midas Touch too late.

Tenderness is gone; the game is at its end,
  the truth cuts deep. No lies are left to defend.
Outcast you've become from those you once held dear,
  you tread the fragile line between hatred and fear.
Uncertainty creases your brow with pleats of woe;
  the proverb proves true: "You reap what you sow."
Cry as you will, but tears won't erase the toll.
  The chaos you caused proves revenge is best served cold.
Hatred burns, its fire offers no release,
  its torment the fruit of a harvest devoid of peace.

There you have it; take it or leave it,
the truth laid bare, a bittersweet seed.
Plant it in your heart, or let it bleed.
Through the ripples of what we've done,
a harsh truth rises from chaos spun,
bouncing through life in a merciless loop.
Love, pain, or pleasure, together or apart,
this question lingers, etched in my heart:
Do we all possess this Midas Touch?
Will every life we touch become as much?

Sensations of Becoming

Life sows seeds of unease in the shrine of existence,
each sprout a paradox, stitched by irony's needle.
Frustration germinates in the soil of adversity,
and every corner turned reveals another puzzle.

Growth plays in the dark as stems reach high,
emerging as fleeting bursts of triumph.
Sparks of love, joy, and hope,
like stars in a moonless sky,
illuminating the path of this weary shoot.

Though vibrations elicit shivers of fear,
heed their lessons, nonetheless.
Hardship, adversity, affliction, and trials;
treacherous yet wise, they sculpt and refine,
carving the soul with the chisel of experience.

Every lesson engraved onto the canvas of life
is a precious gem mined from its deepest caverns.
These are the heirlooms of wisdom,
treasured gifts passed down through time's river.

So cling to your primal and cogitated sensations;
those bittersweet relics of our substance,
in whose veiled grasp lies the crux of existence.
A dance with man, a voyage with gods and demons.

Here, in the delicate balance of allure and fear,
death's tentacles either ensnare or unfetter our souls.
A shocking revelation, a subliminal truth:
in enlightenment's core, darkness blooms.

Tender as Thorns

Wounded by your denial, an assault on my soul,
tears swell in my heart; my eyes burn with pain.
Will I vanish like a dream or haunt like a silhouette?
Separation looms heavy over the edge of our horizon.
Your words about him echo in my mind;
your admiration for his strength, shin, and thigh
diminishes me; a dissolving halo in your sight.
No longer can I endure your hollow excuses,
your deceitful caresses, your venomous kiss.

The façade of honeyed words, once my solace,
has become a torment, a waking nightmare.
I thought of leaving, not once, not twice,
but the thought of your absence aged my soul.
My heart clung to illusions tighter than reality;
living without you felt like an impossible climb.
Your allure, once sweet, now only brings agony.
I planted a garden of love, only to watch it wither.
The truth dawns, cold, bare, and brutal:
your heart belongs to another!
Go, pursue your desire.
But heed this: life always balances the scales,
One day, you, too, shall sip from this bitter chalice.

Your goodbye twists like a knife in my chest.
It falls like stones, shattering what's left of me.
This parting, I didn't choose, but I won't stop you.
Not this time. Loving you should not feel like this.
My eyes are open to the charades you've played;
from your heartless grip, I will find liberation.
No longer will you control the course of my life.
And remember this, my once-beloved:
life will always reciprocate.

Let Go

In a garden of shared dreams and divided hopes,
souls wander, tangled in fate's indifferent loops,
as bards hum woefully, voices parched with longing.
At his side, a grace once radiant
feels as distant as a star slipping from sight.
They witness life's countless struggles,
yet each second marks their declining bond.
Their love, once a typhoon, is losing its volume;
from a language of glances to the absence of caresses.

Their lives a symphony of laughter turned lament
hold the thirst for a love that no longer quenches.
A union once seamless now frays at the edges,
pussivanting through their waning connection,
a bellwether to the final refrain and I,
the bard, compose this requiem of undoing,
mourning the specter of a love not yet buried.

I know the confusion and hardship you sometimes face,
draw courage from the strength you carry within.
Every hardship wanes; even sorrow passes.
Each moment ripens in its destined hour;
all things find meaning and reason in their time.
And you are a gift, wrapped with care
and sealed with love.

Cherish those who cherish you,
preserve the love you are given.
Rekindling this bond may foster a lasting voyage;
one that tempts, teases, fulfills, and appeases,
quenching the soul's deepest longing.

Do not surrender your joy to that which threatens it.
Remain the beautiful soul you are
always faithful, ever kind.

Yes! Rest your pain-brushed heart in my embrace.

Here, let your sorrows freely flow,
like a stream maturing into a river,
nourishing life in its wake.

Ah, breathe! Relish the relief that comes with tears.
Isn't it strangely beautiful?

Laugh! Let your love cascade.
Let it flow, flow—rising with your heartbeats,
a current of compassion, reason, and serenity.
Watch as your mind awakens to clarity.

Can you feel my love washing over your being,
filling you with delight born of pure love?
I dream of you sharing this with me,
basking in love's liberating freedom.
Do not fear to show your love.
Let it be seen, let it be felt.
In its expression lies a true bliss
beyond the grasp of words.

And still, fighting for your love,
I lose myself, piece by piece.
In the bard's tongue, I sing a bittersweet reprise:
love is most often confessed in the season of parting.
My prayers, more fervent than the bereaved for the dying,
and more pious than a sinner seeking salvation,
rise in the ache of love's departure.
Whether shaped by fate, fault, or neither,
love finds its clearest voice
in the weight of its absence.

A Peek into the Past

I look up, only to be caught in the velvet fire of her eyes.
She beckons, subtly yet compellingly.
Captivated, I follow her trail with clandestine steps.
Drawn into her orbit, my resistance fades.
Trance-like, I follow, desire my chain.
Her hypnotic smile, laced with promise,
leads me along a path of mystery;
caught like a feather in the wind, I float.

Willingly, I'm steered to realms of ecstasy;
a dreamer adrift in waves of delight.
Transported to an isle of enchantment,
I cruise, eyes wide with wonder.
Familiar faces, unchanged by time, greet me.
They remain youthful, forever eleven,
while decades etch their lines upon my skin.
Is this a portal to death or heaven's door?
Time ebbs, youth surges anew, to relive longings,
joys, and desires too intense for words,
the succulent fruits of forbidden memory;
mine to savor, to enjoy, to treasure.
In this haven of bliss, I am moored.
Here, I could linger until life's end.

But as she smiled, I recognized her face at last.
Not a lover. A ghost. Something long buried.

The illusion shatters, a veil torn wide;
reality unveils its macabre vignettes.
I fall, unprepared, into depths I thought I'd erased;
a ghastly vista, harsh and unforgiving.
Darkness descends, viscerally real,
a raw and unfiltered nightmare unfolds.

Shots ring out, an assault on the soul;
    I am shot at, attacked,
        and emotionally shattered.
      I am raped, chased,
          and savagely degraded.

This thing that's happening, I wish undone;
This nightmare unspooling, a horror unwelcome.
In my fright, I cry, "Save me, Lord!"
A plea for salvation in the face of despair.
Defiance writhes within me; I battle to break free,
straining to escape the grasp of its onslaught.

With every ounce of strength, I lunge forward,
plummeting over the edge of my bed.
My eyes snap open, my heart a riotous thunder.
I awake. The past still breathes inside me;
a harrowing reminder of what I survived.

Willed into Wakefulness

Our minds are directors of motion pictures;
stunning realities hidden in the matrix of dreams.
They feel real yet vanish at dawn's first gleam,
leaving us startled by reveries
that disrupt and shatter our slumber.

In those fleeting moments of hypnagogia,
we grasp at the threads of our torpid utopia,
pondering, perhaps jotting down fragments.
The allure of sleep's hazy embrace
proves more tempting than recording dreams.

Dreams are the pulse of possibility, of what could be.
They pull us in with primal magnetism.
We are coaxed to ignite the power within,
dispel the fog of lethargy,
and render compromise obsolete.

Their energy, a catalyst for passion,
tunes our destinies to clearer frequencies.
Some dreams pacify with benign currency,
offering refuge from the harshness of reality
and numbing the soul's most persistent aches.

At daybreak, clarity sharpens our sight.
We learn to separate the imagined from the real.
These night-born visions uncover daily dilemmas,
unspoken yearnings and unmet needs.
Through dreams, alternate realms offer wisdom,
urging us to listen, bidding us to heed.

Dreams hold sway.
We bow to them or bend them to our will,
a delicate dance between surrender and control.
Breaking free requires intention,
an act of will or self-preservation.

Within dreamscapes, dystopias often hide:
obstacles, people, and possessions
competing to hinder, entrap, or conquer.
Yet with purpose aligned and vision clear,
we vanquish the ghosts that haunt our path.

As we descend through the strata of the psyche,
dreams offer more than riddles or retreat.
They bear the weight of soulwork left unfinished,
initiations unspooling in night's reels and scripts,
each step a summons to become more fully awake.

A Lament

Kin, can you hear the screams of my soul?
Muffled cries at dawn, a heart's bitter toll.
A spirit parched in deserts unholy,
a form now shattered, far from its goal.

Witness, O world, with your eyes open wide:
dwellings crumble, derided, and cast aside.
Hearts long for solace, souls disheartened,
and flesh cries for *bread*, yet it is denied.

Do you perceive me, O people of Earth?
Wandering lands far from my birth,
a spectrum of hues, rich and unsung,
beyond the bounds of the rainbow's girth.

Hear me, O Spirit, Breath of the Fusion,
grant us the sight to pierce delusion.
In a world where phantoms wear human skin,
and truths worse than reality hold no illusions.

Lead us to clarity beyond immaculate grails
through life's storm and its formidable gales,
where illusions are worse than the real,
and hearts bleed light that flickers, dims, and fails.

We, your children, in difference spun,
reach for justice beneath the same sun.
Though fractured now, can we still be one,
or are the threads already undone?

Cold

Our interaction lacks the spark of human connection.
Speaking with you feels constrained, robotic.
Words processed like data from a screen.
Cold. Detached.
Are you a creature, or something else entirely?
Your lifeless responses leave only questions,
and I'm left parsing silence for what's never there.

I've grown frigid; a shield against losing again,
a defense forged when my father walked out.
Two decades later, I've weathered too much.
Countless faces entered my life,
only to vanish without warning.
This emotional frost is not of my making.

Society's callous grip constricts my chest.
My heart, bruised, wrung out, cast aside.
I've been mistreated by those I dared to trust.
I was a friend to her, to him, to many,
offering guidance like a clockwork mentor.
I watched them arrive. Then came the goodbyes,
each farewell carving me colder than the last.
Now I live in the chill of departure:
crushed. Numb. Unfeeling.

Killing with Innocence

This is not murder.
It's an unhinged mania.
Not cruelty, but stark realism:
a predator's instinct to kill,
lest it be killed.

Stealthy as a jackal stalking prey,
you watch its elegance wilt and fade,
then strike with a ruthless *coup de grâce*.

This isn't a mere mental breakdown.
It's a deep-seated psychosis,
welcomed inside.
Disguised in innocence, a lamb in form,
but serpent-like in strike and aim.

Honeyed words mask venomous intent,
a scout for danger hot on the trail.
It hunts in stealth, patient and precise,
killing without hesitation.
This is not mere malefic intent,
but a vindictive and perilous plot.

With cunning and care,
you crafted your scheme.
With innocence and diligence,
you cast your spell.
And with surgical precision,
you dissected and dismembered.

Blood seeps, then trickles,
gushes, then spurts.
The heart stutters and gasps,
clinging to its final breath.
Your closing blow lands
with icy precision
sealing the execution in cold finality.

This is not happenstance,
it is deliberate retribution
Not mere skepticism,
but a step across the threshold,
retaliation for the torment endured.
If caught in the spell,
unable to break free,
your mind and body
will be destroyed—discarded.

Rejected

You awaken the beast within me.
My hair bristles, sharp as quills.
My body roars, a lion claiming its domain.
And like an eagle locking sights on its prey,
my focus is riveted on you.
      Yet, beneath your piercing gaze,
          I am subdued.

You stir nature's fury inside me.
A latent force erupts like a volcano,
exploding from the depths of infernal purgatory.
It flows like molten lava, an *Eburnean* eruption,
its ivory heat consuming all in its searing path.
      Yet beneath your frosty stare,
          I freeze in place.

You invoke the serpent in me.
Like a cobra, I hiss and unfurl,
gliding forward, revealing my form.
Eager, I glide toward your cavern,
      but under your scrutiny,
          I slither away.

You summon the storm in me.
Rain-laden clouds, a tempest brewing.
My thundering heart a harbinger of unrest.
Like lightning's strike, raw energy flashes,
a deluge of emotions, wild and fierce.
      But under your glare,
          I fall silent, utterly spent.

The Ruin You Left

They walk by, holding hands,
staring into each other's eyes,
and our past rises like smoke from embers.
Their laughter slices through me;
a sharp pain in the desolate chambers of my heart.
Life has not ended, though it feels like it should,
and in some ways, it has.
Still, I must breathe,
inhale this melancholic air.

I lose myself in daily tasks,
hoping they will dull the shards of memory,
so I won't feel your absence, heavy, oppressive,
a gnawing void lodged in the corners of my soul.

There are moments, like this morning,
when I don't want to go on,
when darkness threatens to swallow me whole.
Tonight, your ghost will visit my sleep,
a cruel reminder of the boundaries of love.
Did you ever exist, or was it all a dream?
You've been gone so long,
becoming a phantom in the corridors of my mind.

Will I ever truly live again?
Who can I tell? Who would understand?
My grief is like a night without dawn.
People keep telling me to move on,
but my life was built around you.
Now that you're gone, I am ruined,
a relic of the past,
adrift in the tides of today's sorrow.

Where I Was Left to Break

I sacrificed so much for your comfort,
bearing the loss, enduring the hurt.
For all the kindness I showed to ease your pain,
you shattered my hopes and left only strain.

When you bid farewell, my chest grew hollow,
tears fell freely as I drowned in sorrow.
Day and night, I reached out in despair,
hoping you'd answer, show that you care.

My texts and emails met only silence,
leaving me questioning my self-reliance.
Was I a clown in a tragic play, a pitiable fool,
trapped by our love and cruelly schooled?

In sadness, I gaze at the sky and sigh.
Once I sang your praise, now I cry.
I often spoke of how good you'd been to me,
but now, when asked, I want to flee.

For all the things you said to me,
all the vows you made, were they meant to be?
Your broken promises pierced my heart with ease,
leaving wounds so deep, no remedy can appease.

If I should die today, it won't be by human hands,
nor nature's fury, nor time's demand.
It would be the pain inside, an emotional disarray.
Was I a fool or simply blind?
I bow my head and cry.

Words from a Broken Heart

In my mind, a hurricane of thoughts is raging wild.
Words flow like rivers, by sorrow defiled,
hidden in my soul, aching to be known,
muted by a world that chills to the bone.

My desperate pleas pierce the dying light.
In this deafening world, who heeds my plight?
Shards of delight, once soaring like birds,
lie shattered, transformed by jagged words.

Rejection's poisoned arrow, persecution's icy gaze,
ever-present guides through life's perplexing maze.
Chasing passion and pleasure in a game of strife,
I am left adrift, forever questioning life.

Pens bleed; keys weep, my heart's a delirious ballad.
There's healing in this verse, though the pain is valid.
My soul is heavy with sorrow unexpressed,
and in my thoughts, death gains steady access.

In cycles of despair, turning like planets in orbit;
even my faith in God, I'm tempted to forfeit.
Sweet words spoken with a forked tongue hide a viper's nest;
each step through my mind feels like a spear in my chest.

Am I a prisoner of my thoughts, lost in my own hell?
Stripped of rest, my invocation is no longer, "It is well."
For by the rivers of time, sad memories beset,
leaving me weary of life's inquisition and regret.

Wearied from the battles ceaselessly fought,
I falter where reason and anguish are caught.
In this restless flow of life, I find I don't belong;
alone, I trace the discord that prolonged the wrong.

A Love Not Mine to Hold

Loving you is an ache that began with a glance.
Emotional cords connected through a hug,
a resonance of something almost said.
It's a dagger plunging into my ribs,
a bittersweet tether pulling at its cage,
binding me to a love I cannot claim.

I carry your tears like a fragile relic,
hammering against the walls of my heart.
Your voice exhales in the corridors of my solitude,
you're a vanishing form I cannot touch.

You live in the space between my reach and the stars,
in stolen glances that carve new wounds,
in words I craft and dare not speak.
You are the mirage of an oasis,
close enough to thirst for,
but distant enough to leave me parched.

I offered you love, pure, raw, unguarded
only to see it reflected as confusion,
a riddle instead of the desired communion.
It's said we moved through different seasons,
a divide too wide to cross.
That our story, carved by time,
could not find a home in your horizon.

You said I wasn't what you needed,
that my key was cut for a different lock.
My edges don't align with your design.
Your tone firm and dismissive,
a scalpel separating possibility from hope.
And still, I waver, aching for you
knowing I am not the shape in your dreams.

And then there were these words:
"Chemistry," as if love were nothing but science.
"Worth," as if value could be counted in offerings.
I was reduced to absence and currency,
left aching in a dial tone of memory.

I walk in rhythms of psalmists,
while your heart clings to altars you designed.
I never sought to pull you with the gravity of my belief,
for some distances are woven by choices
no hand can make or unmake.

Yet the worst distress, the heart's true breaking,
was not in what was withheld
but in what I still carried.
The ripple of your sobs in my thoughts,
the embrace that felt like home
for that brief forever,
erased as if it had never been.

You answer for others:
calls, laughter, effortless connection.
But for me, the line remains severed.
Your silence is a blade pressed into my being,
a grief that sighs, not enough, never enough.

And yet, I remain *vulnerable* yet wise.
I choose to be kind, to be gentle,
to hold your name in my prayers
even as your absence tears me apart.
For love, even unreturned, is still sacred.

There's a certain resilience in this,
a serene, undeclared strength.
It cradles my complex grief,
kisses the thorn as it bleeds,
and loves even in the absence of love.

But oh, the jealousy stings like salt in a wound,
to see you give to others
what you keep from me.
And yet, I do not sever the cord,
for even in this pain, there is something holy.
I will not harden. I will not hate.
This ache is my Eucharist;
a love feast of grief I dare to receive.

In the hunger that wells beneath composure,
I've unmoored myself,
dismantling boundaries I swore to keep,
a reckless lunge into the arms of fate
for the chance to be gathered into something human.

Still, I cherish this brokenness,
for it reveals the depth of my heart,
a heart capable of holding both love and pain,
a heart that wept, "I miss you"
even as it learns to let you go...

I will not build walls from this.
I will not let bitterness become my second skin.
If you need your space,
I will grant it with grace.
Even if our bond dissolves without a word,
and what we called friendship thins into air,
I will find solace in my inner cross,
whose axis pulses in Eucharistic sorrow
I will still stand ready,
open to a love that might one day
choose me back.

This, too, is love.
The unanswered kind,
the desire that burns within our chest,
a bruise you trace with burning tears,
because even in pain, it is yours,
and even in absence, it is real.

You are the ache I will carry.
I will carry this hurt, not as a wound
but like a chimerical shard,
wounding but not piercing,
a symbol of determination,
of a heart that dared to love
in the hope of possessing something
it cannot have.

No Space Between Us

She called him her blessing,
her whole world.
He grew up learning
to answer her pain
before his scraped knees bled.

His joy was hers to manage.
She filled his silences
with her voice,
read his moods
like weather: stalling, surging,
fast then slow
always pulling from his pulse
while forecasting storms
he never chose.

There was no door
between their hearts,
only a narrow stage
where long-planted strings
ran through his limbs
pulling tighter
each time he tried
to stage his own show.

He wanted to be good.
So he stayed close,
shared everything,
carried her loneliness
like an inherited throne.

Until love arrived,
and she flinched.
He named someone else sacred
and she felt betrayed.

She never said,
don't go,
but her eyes glinted
with the weight
of all she thought he owed
every guilt
his spine could carry.

Now, when he tries to leave,
he carries her voice in his soul.
The one that says,
you are mine, even when you're gone.

He wonders
if freedom means disloyalty
if his first yes to someone else
was also his first exile.
Will peace mean absence?
Can love live
without sacrifice?

He longs to return—
not to her
but to the part of him
that was once his alone.

High on Emptiness

The music brews its magic as bodies collide,
lost in rhythm, gliding, grinding in time.
DJs, conductors of the night and sorcerers of sound
conjure beats that stir the booty shakers
while bartenders summon potions in the dim-lit haze.
Lovers and strangers savor forbidden desire,
fruit tasted in stolen moments.
They cuddle and kiss, plotting escapes
amid echoes of laughter in this euphonic haven,
where stories are written in the language of longing.

The night's enchantment loosens its grip,
leaving only the weight of reality.
The music, once a festive fiend,
now fades to a waning heartbeat.
The shakers, the scenes, lose their luster.
The crowd's fervor feels fractured,
like pieces of a puzzle no one stayed to finish.

It's time to call it a night,
heed the siren call to solitude.
In this sea of strangers, I sought refuge from seclusion,
yet loneliness, that unwelcome companion, lingers,
a weight on my heart, a witness to my vulnerability.
Amid fleeting glances and transient encounters,
I search for a connection that evades and eludes,
leaving my heart wandering in melancholic tension.

The farewell of lovers and the drifting of friends
imprints a sadness that settles and overwhelms.
Is the absence of romance a sign of defect?
This invites social displeasure, a sense of shame.
Every sexual climax leaves me more depleted than before.
Is there a path out of this valley of the forsaken?
Do we choose loneliness, or does it choose us?

Hurt and abandoned because she chose her.
In the company of others, I thought only of you,
and in solitude, he wonders and ponders about him.
As depression looms, I crave something more.
This unfillable void becomes impossible to ignore.

Oh, whatever you do, don't lose your head.
She has no spouse, and he has an empty bed.
The changing of companions wears me thin;
its sting draws tears like slicing onions.
I step from the club, feigning elation,
a lonely soul with a heart of desperation.
I enter my sanctuary and dim the light.
Cold sheets greet my skin in an unshared bed.
I toss and turn, heat rising where a touch should be,
igniting a sadness that sinks into despair.

As the night drapes me in its velvet cloak,
slumber beckons, offering a transient reprieve.
When the new dawn rises, another tide of trials awaits,
ready to pierce my heart as it tries to recover.
Once again, I will search for a suitor,
to share life's highs, to endure its lows,
and to pursue, once more, a better forever.

Wounds Time Cannot Erase

I reflect on my prison, its walls spanning a lifetime,
a fortress built from stone and inner fears alike.
A home surrounded by a community of bars,
where norms clip wings and traditions deter.
A country that feels like a confining cell,
curtailing dreams with riveting éclat.
The most persistent jailer of all lies within:
self-made barriers that impede and stall.
The thought of returning to these familiar confines
sends a sliver of dread slicing through me.
There, words and views act as suffocating hosts.
To return feels like slipping into a noose,
where my truest self bends against its will.
To be known would have meant exile.
For had they known who kindled desires in my chest,
or in whose arms I sought solace from their tyranny,
I would have been cast out,
left to sleep on the streets,
abandoned to the gutters.
This secret I carried for years.
It roamed my mind, seeking ways to escape.
My somatic reactions betrayed me often.
At times, I thought I was having a mental breakdown.
Something in me longed for liberation.
Lust broke my chains, and the Earth trembled in reply.
The mountain hid its fire, yet Lotharios found my heart.
The test was not my desire
but my hunger.
My bite, a rebellion.
His surrender, complacency.
If I reached for freedom, then who forged these chains?

Memories of abuse clawed back with sharp intent;
chilling scenes from the past besieged my mind.
My heart cracked like thunder,
yet still no one listened.
I recalled schoolmates expelled for wearing earrings.
Gay children cast out by parents
who'd sacrificed everything for their schooling.
One image still haunts me: a young woman abused,
shot down in a bustling square for being lesbian.
Her blood pooled crimson as she hit the ground.
The images linger:
friends weeping in fear,
hunkered low and helpless,
writhing in agony,
as family, friends, and strangers struck them.
Slurs "homos," "dykes," "freaks,"
burned like venom from countless tongues.
Sermons invoke hellfire, damnation,
demonic possession, and perverse temptation.
These words, like acid, seared the ears.
Deejays flooded the airwaves with tunes
calling for murder, stoking cheers.
With political fervor, officials proclaimed:
"Not in my Cabinet."
Brick by brick, we built walls of exclusion.
These are the memories engraved in my heart.
The evidence of wounds
that time cannot erase.

Experiencing a Crack Concert

Retreating from winter's biting grasp, I tumble indoors,
into the mall's bustling cacophony.
A universe alive with its quirky rhythms.
Consumerism hums a hypnotic tune;
merchandise gleaming beneath holiday lights.
The crowd moves like puppets on invisible strings,
their eyes wandering like children, wide with awe.

I wonder. Is there still a pandemic?

Phssssss, brrrap, brrrap, brrrap.
A discordant note splits the air,
unexpected and raw, yet oddly fitting.
It disrupts the mall's melody with its unplanned song.

Thwap, thwap, thwap, ssssppp.
A fleeting moment of levity.
I glance around like a spy on a mission,
searching for the rowdy bandit.
I'm not one to be shy.

My grandmother always had a word
whenever we started showing off in public.
"Don't toot your own horn," she'd say.
But sometimes you must let off *hot wind,*
lest people think you are a *tushy tickler.*

I still haven't pinpointed the source of the sounds,
but soon, the lingering evidence betrays the culprit.
The bandit is me!

Freedom courses through my whole being,
from the crown of my head to my soles.
The scent of *baking brownies, air tulips,*
and charred wood slowly infuses the air.

Poot, poot, poot— ab-so-lute-ly free speech!
One knows the feeling of an empty stomach,
but this is not hunger pangs;
it's delightfully freeing.

The whiff that pervaded the air earlier
is now a heady aroma.
The rhythmic, thundering *clap, clap, clap,*
brrr-ing, tingles the tail, telling a tale
of a *mouse on a motorcycle.*

I look around to see if there's an audience,
any witnesses to my *crack concert.*
With lustered cheeks,
I pray those behind are at least six feet,
and their masks are made of more than one sheet.

Not in the least perturbed by the epic
thunder from down under, I maintain my dignity
and murmur the maxim:
"Behind every great fart, there is a great behind."

Ice

The tears in my eyes are frozen still;
my cheeks, hard as steel, endure the chill.
The blood surging through my veins
carries a fiery cold that can quell an inferno.

My tendons and ligaments, crisp as new banknotes,
stand rigid, like a tree trunk buried in crystal snow.
My skin, tight as a drum's taut hide,
lets frosty breath escape from deep inside.

In my presence, the cosmos turns mournfully gray;
even the sun hesitates, fearful of casting its rays.
Its heat cannot break this cryopathic spell
as raindrops freeze, suspended where they fell.

Everything I touch grows lifeless, cold.
Tears long to flow, to be released,
but they are trapped in a wintry sea.
For you, my tears and I remain frozen in fate;
hard as gold, a living statue.
I'm held in rejection's grip,
an eternal winter, never to thaw.

Gathering the Shards

If the previous sections wrestled with the play of power, politics, loss, and longing, this final act speaks of survival and what it means to be made new without erasing what was. These poems do not offer platitudes or easy answers. Instead, they offer perspective, an embrace of contradiction, a reverence for the scars we carry, and the hope that springs from resilience.

Here, the poems walk with humility. They laugh, heal, honor, and reflect. They draw upon nature, memory, ancestry, and divine breath. Growth appears not as triumph but as process, one that includes missteps, confessions, affirmations, and grace. This is the part of the journey where the shattered pieces begin to shine again. Not because they are fixed, but because they are seen and perhaps even loved.

The Little Things We Take for Granted

The pungency of my crack concert trails behind me,
an odorous alchemy uniquely mine.
I step deeper into the mall's busy terrain,
my eyes drinking in the vibrant, enticing sights.

Shops shine like lighthouses of desire,
promising financial fiascos for those
not in malice with their wallets.
For penny-pinchers, it's a dance with danger.
For the affluent, it is a chess game with their gold.
And for those less flush, it's a tightrope act,
balancing compulsion and common sense.

Cheerful guides strike poised stances at shop entries,
armed with sanitizers, shields, and uneasy smiles,
eager to nudge shoppers toward indulgence.
Modern sentinels of an age we'd prefer to forget,
they stand as solemn reminders of our altered reality.

Somewhere in my mind, my friend's words echo:
"The hardest part isn't the isolation of the ICU;
it's not being able to hold hands with your loved ones."
The thought hangs heavy, even here,
in this temple of consumerism.

I exhale in relief upon reaching the food court.
Thankfully, it's not packed.
Patrons sit apart, their tables a mosaic of space,
each piece placed by the hands of caution.

Suddenly, a melodious *trouser trumpet* commences;
a symphony felt more in the soul than heard by the ears.
An *anus applause*, the song of living organisms.
Buurrrpp. An abrupt expelling of air
punctuates the performance.

Surely, the pleasure of chewing gum
isn't the reason for this burping tantrum.
Perhaps the sight of the food court
is the brigand behind this bodily out-breath.
I detour.
The gift shop beckons, and I stray,
trading gum for candy, postponing lunch.

"Things come in threes," or so they claim.
Thankfully, I've yet to encounter the fourth.
But soon, my new indulgence betrays me.
Hic-hic-hic—rapid, relentless, resounding.

I spit out the candy, and soon my chest heaves with relief.
Just as quickly as they came, the hiccups vanish.
I glance around, relieved to find everyone
too preoccupied to notice my *Bronx cheer*.
My grand act drew no side-eyes, no head turns.
Not even a smirk to mark my moment of glory.

Indeed, things come in threes, like sneezes,
disasters, and my questionable decisions.
Still unbothered, I march into the gift shop.
The scene that greets me is cinematic.

A young lady sneezes. Just once.
Time slows, the air thick with suspense.
Then chaos erupts!
Baskets fly, shoppers scattering like startled pigeons.

Turning to flee, a young man collides
with an elderly woman, both falling flat on their bums.
Masked and shielded, cashiers dive for cover
behind their counters.
For a moment, the chaos
is so intense you might believe a terrorist
had strapped explosives to a shopping cart.

I fumble for my phone to capture the frenzy.
Alas, I'm too late. The action dissolves
before I can seize it.

The lady stands, bewildered, as onlookers gather.
I stare, amazed. My own triadic masterpieces.
The butt percussion, eructation tantrum,
and singultus solo hadn't drawn a fraction
of this commotion.
A singular sneeze stole the show,
proving once and for all, timing is everything.

Joyful Bitterness

Life is a labyrinth of labor and loss,
where woes weave an obscure cross.
Hardships pile high, an avalanche of rubble.
Will they lead us to joy or deeper trouble?

What's felt today is what the past dictates;
your choices today shape tomorrow's state.
In a tranquil heart, does anguish hide,
or, amid death's chaos, is suffering denied?

In the abyss of distress and darkness, we grope,
seeking inspiration, a glimmer of hope,
to mend the cracks of a fragile mind.
Have faith in yourself, or life will be unkind.

With faith and will, we confront our nightmares.
Cease chasing the fleeting, the things that ensnare.
To live is not an illusion we yearn to possess
but a chimerical web where we pursue happiness.

Blessings are sought and claimed by those who thirst,
tugging destiny's strings, their fortunes reversed.
Not mere ideas of the mind, but earned and seized
by those who yearn, their anguish appeased.

In Retrospect: Call, Raise, or Fold

The world rejoiced at the child's birth, save for one.
The path ahead was shrouded in mystery,
awaiting the brushstrokes of experience,
shaped in the fog of uncertainty and becoming.

Life is like a card game; the cards initially dealt,
and through ominous omens, life's tests began.
As stakes rose, victories and losses were called.
The dealers win most in the casino of existence,
leaving punters content with modest gains.

Aggression, aggravation, deprivation, and evolution
began to mark the child in signs clearly visible.
A queen from the pack, a queer narrative projected.
With intrigue and wild reverie, friends became models,
tied to doorknobs and playfully flogged.

Mischief held meaning; it was thought-provoking,
as some were caught on knees gyrating.
In those days, there were no tapes. No recordings.
But as time advanced, life fashioned its form;
even doorknob frolics burned with raw intensity.

The method was there, meaning to the madness.
Emotions coalesced as life spun its complex tapestry.
Young love, at seven, twelve, and thirteen,
left a trail of scars and a chorus of remarks.
The needle threaded pain: abuse, bias, becoming.

A career was chosen; a new chapter began.
In sadness and seclusion, life lost its rhythm.
The child left home; destiny reshuffled the deck.
Resources waned; no income expected.
A stranger's floor became a refuge from despair.

Betrayal's sting burned, bleak and distressing.
Arrested in a case of mistaken identity;
A red suit to blame, harmless in design,
yet revealing scenes that chilled to the bone.

The detention room became a stage for harsh truths.
A child sacrificed on the altar of justice,
victim of laws meant to protect.
The system defecates on its own ideals,
drowning innocence in a sea of pretense.

By some stroke of luck, a hand was exposed.
Two tens, one three. Fortune flirted, then folded.
Life's wager continued, the deck reshuffled again.
Quickly, love ignited, then turned to embers,
and healing followed, slow but inevitable.

Lust, a fever in the bloodstream, rising hot, hot, hot,
blinding reason, searing hearts with reckless heat.
Escape required a web of deceit,
where lies and labels became the only truths I knew.
Two jacks, two deuces, and an ace in hand.
The stakes demand a choice:
to call, to raise, or to fold.

The casino's tables yielded to the ripples of a pool,
fruitful yet fraught with bitter deceptions,
capturing moments and refining experiences.
Its allure blinded both the wary and the wise,
pulling all into its seductive plots and promises.

Yet the game remains incomplete:
three sevens, two deuces,
a full house laid bare.
In pondering the past,
one thing is certain:
all that was is,
and all that is was.

In retrospect, the cards we hold
become the scars we wear;
each marking a story,
each a testament to survival,
for the root of our pain is the absence of gain.

Behind the Smile

I have not had time to savor the roses' perfume,
their fading scent, like my joy, is diffused by your words.
Words that are like daggers, ruthless, piercing,
plunging me into agony and anguish.
To protect my wounded dignity, I wear a smile,
a façade to mask my pain.
Behind my hurt, despair floods like persistent rain.
Make no mistake, these are not smiles of joy!
They conceal the wounds you've inflicted,
an ongoing, melancholic flow of tears;
things I won't ask you to understand.
Your deeds and cruel incantations linger,
like an invisible wraith that haunts,
their impact, leaving a lasting scathe.

Pause and Ponder

I wonder why spurned affection wounds so deeply.
Sadness, horror, and disgrace consume completely.
Its peculiar nature is both eerie and bizarre;
its absence leaves an open, bleeding scar,
festering in rumination, resentment, reprisal.

The poet ponders why the grass is green
and wonders why the wind remains unseen.
I, too, reflect on life's intricate vignettes.
The grass and wind scheming to compose a dirge,
and the earth paints answers we already know.

What about you? Do you ponder the same?
What secrets haunt your mind and name?
Has the wind breathed words you dare not speak?
I ponder the ways of life, its peculiar flow.
How people give in to woeful throes,
pawns in the grand tragedy of existence.

I often ponder the art of friendship and its making.
I extend the open hand of fellowship,
only to discover a one-sided connection.
Alas, I befriend, but am I befriended?
Still I give, offering more than I receive.

I always wonder if I am truly loved.
They say I am beloved of the divine,
but that is not the love my heart seeks.
Lo, I realize it is I who have loved,
yet never have I been your beloved.

Ever feel like hell's broken loose around you?
Well, I do. I do. I truly do!
This isn't just hell on Earth;
it's a purgatory I cannot escape,
a fire that scorches but refuses to consume.

And there it is, undeniable, stark, and clear:
love's absence is like slipping off the edge.
For in the place where love does not dwell,
the absence of love is the presence of hell.

A Child's Honor

My claim is simple: You are beyond compare!
In the annals of motherhood,
you are a singular phenomenon.
A mother like you is once in a lifetime,
and never shall the world know another.

You braved life's merciless storms,
facing each challenge with resolute courage,
without a murmur of grievance or complaint.
The tears you shed, silent and selfless,
fell not for yourself
but for us, your children.

Your hands, etched with tales of toil,
bear the memory of tireless labor.
Your back, a testament to resilience,
has borne the weight of countless bends;
the heft of life's unyielding burdens.
The earth drank the sweat of your brow;
a nurturing elixir that sustained our lives.

Your feet traversed distant frontiers
to shield us from the world's cruelty,
shaping our spirits to endure its trials.
You forfeited your days selflessly
so our nights could be cradles of comfort.
You are my oasis in a barren desert,
the root from which my branches grew strong.
You stood firm when others faltered,
a constant in an ever-shifting, hostile world.

Your silence and deeds speak louder than words,
a sonata of unspoken love and sacrifice.
Today, I lift my praise in homage to you,
for the life you built with love as your creed.
I stand in awe of your boundless strength,
a rare force of nature: my mother,
my eternal pillar of strength and love.

The Other Side

On the other side of hate, love embraces the despised.
On the other side of doubt lies abiding faith.
On the other side of darkness, light reveals a path.
On the other side of a frown, a smile waits.
On the other side of love, I see only you.
On the other side of work is sweet reward and rest.
On the other side, faded grass always seems greener.
On the other side of envy, goodwill takes root.

To believe the other side of life is always better
is folly whispering in inexperienced ears.
From afar, the boundless forest blurs—
a lone tree on the horizon masquerades as plenty.
No journey is endless.
No sorrow eternal.
There is no day without night.
No darkness without light.
It's funny how we look to the other side,
seeing things not as they are,
mistaking illusions for treasures
at times, appreciating feces as gold.

From a distance, even a puddle looks like a stream.
A silhouette can make simple things beautiful,
and edges blend in harmony.
On the other side, danger seems harmless,
and the vilest of threats is only a thought.
On the other side, everything seems different,
but not always as it truly is.

Walk

When the sun hides its light,
I'll still walk with dignity!
And when the moon turns black,
I'll walk in faith!

Though solitude is my companion
and the days grow dismal,
in stillness, I find strength,
and the path, though uncertain, becomes clear.

I will use the tears from my cheeks
to satisfy my thirst for victory.
Then, I will use my faith to satisfy
my deep longing for peace.

When hope is in chaos,
and flames threaten to consume the world,
when fear shrouds our existence,
I'll press toward the purpose for which I'm called.

I am committed to the sacred.
I will let no one deter me from this path.
For they say, "Alone you were born,
and alone you will die."

But I proclaim,
"Yes, alone I was born,
and with Christ, I shall die."

Be Positive

Feelings and values are like the ocean's tides;
changing and shifting, but never to be denied.
Accept your lot, yourself, and the truth.
Become the change you long to see.

The currents of growth flow within and without;
letting go is the path to freedom.
First, speak truth to thyself; to others, do not lie.
The path to virtue is in honesty's reply.

Confront your struggles, insecurities, and pain,
and embrace each failure as a lesson, not in vain.
Hold fast to the grace that hope imparts,
a steady current within our beating hearts.

The courage to forgive is strength, not a flaw,
providing healing beyond this life.
Seek first to understand, then to be understood,
for this principle grounds all that is good.

Celebrate success with humility, not pride,
for arrogance beckons to where demons reside.
Serve others with a heart that's sincere.
No pretense, no malice, only patience and care.

You are the soil where positivity takes root,
a guiding star for wanderers in pursuit.
Pursue your dreams with clear resolutions,
tempered by wisdom, free from delusion.

You are beautifully designed, perfectly created,
crafted to fulfill the intent *Love* has orchestrated.
This one life is yours, so live it right.
Be positive in heart, in spirit, in purpose.

In all you touch and see,
discover your truth, and simply be ...

The Voice of Spring

Spring, the muse of poets, the season of wonder,
awakens the world with promises of new life.
Shoots of hope break through the earth's embrace,
and nature sings in her liveliest tones,
flaunting colors like peacocks in courtship.
Migrant birds revisit their cherished rendezvous,
filling the air with melodies of joy.

In her festive glory, Spring reigns supreme.
A time of change, a bridge to what's yet to be.
She paints the world with what we long to see:
emerald grass stretching far and wide,
flowers blooming in a mirage of colors,
and trees donning crowns of verdant splendor,
saluting the sun's warmer, brighter glow.

Spring showers nourish life from root to bloom,
breathing vigor into flora and fauna.
What once lay dormant now thrives unrestrained.
April showers bring May's beautiful flowers,
and the earth blooms with wild vitality.

Like an infant drawn from the cradle of the womb,
the world exhales its first breath after winter,
greeting the wide, waiting world, alive,
pulsing with wonder and endless possibility.
Every leaf, every beast, a thread tightly spun
in the eternal web of growth and rebirth.

How Things Changed

How long has it been since I last sat here?
Nature has changed, and so has my soul.
This place has seen many tears and sighs.
It has heard and held many of my secrets.

Nature has changed, and so has my soul;
with them, stories that may never be told.
They have heard and held many of my secrets.
It's been a long time since I last sat here.

Stories, indeed, that may never be told;
fantasies: lust, lost love, pain, and regret.
It's been a long time since I last sat here;
I savor the contours of this new romance.

Fantasies: lust, lost love, pain, and regret.
Is this forever love or another short thrill?
I savor the contours of this new romance.
Oh, how things have changed.

Is this forever love or another short thrill?
Doubt tugs at me, yet my heart is full of hope.
Oh, how things have changed;
the peace I'm feeling is so consoling.

Doubt tugs at me, yet my heart is full of hope.
The air is still thick with the scent of melancholy.
But this peace I'm feeling is so consoling.
How long has it been since I last sat here?

The Rhythms of Nature

Nature's splendor stirs the soul in a profound embrace,
the transcendent breaking through the mundane,
unveiling a world of brilliance and wonder.
The soul finds communion with the universe,
a vibrant, living, and interconnected whole.
Ahh, the Divine impulse bestowing authenticity to life!

Life unfurls like butterflies, graceful performers
emerging from chrysalis cloaks.
Once eerie creatures, now radiant with beauty,
glide on rainbowed wings bathed in dawn's light,
a dance that captures and elevates the soul,
bearing witness to life's miraculous transformation.

A distant vibration swells to a crescendo,
the ground trembling at its thunderous roar.
A fiery serpent slashes across the heavens,
its radiance sending shivers through the soul.
In the fusion of sight and sound, awe takes form,
a cathartic euphony awakening the eight senses.

Waves crash in time against shores and reefs,
a harmonious ballet of natural ease.
The sand murmurs songs that ripple through plains,
resonating with nature's rich vibrations.
This is the ocean's rhythm, the cadence of life.

Wind caresses forests. Rain weeps into streams.
The mountains parade strength, and valleys cradle life.
Stars twinkle like watchful eyes as dusk renews their will.

Their breaths flicker in the mist that blankets the Earth,
a synesthetic prelude guiding all life to thrive.

Earth, a nurturing mother, cradles her seeds.
From roots to fruits, flora and fauna worship the sun,
nature weaving existence with mastery and care.
Through her seasons, she teaches patience and grace,
filling our days with bounty; her rhythms in our veins.

In this world of eightfold sense and wonder, I traverse.
Through sight, I marvel at the colors of dawn,
hearing life's cadence in creation's song.
Taste and smell conjure shards of memory and longing,
while touch recalls the warmth that calls my name.
Balance sways with nature's quiet cues,
proprioception anchors me in form and place,
and intuition whispers subtle guidance.

Nature, awakened by a Divine impulse, finds its voice.
Its rhythm echoes through the pulse of life.
The divine spark breathes life with authentic grace,
bearing witness to transformation's wondrous embrace.
A symphony of sensations awakens every sense,
flowing in harmony, the heartbeat of life.

An invisible hand guides life as it flourishes,
her gifts abundant, her rhythms alive within us.

Holy Intimacy

From the heavens, rains of holiness descend,
a blessed cascade nourishing all creation.
In harmonious response, flowers of truth blossom,
and galaxies and horizons mirror and magnify
one another's resplendent beauty.

The universe pulses with a love that binds all things,
seeding acts of righteousness within its design.
It stirs a deep sense of awe and devotion,
as Grace extends her hand, reaching in, reaching out,
delicately touching the core of every soul.

Our hearts thrum with a sacred rhythm,
transcending magic, poetry, and mortal logic,
arising from communion with the Eternal One.
The architect of perpetual fellowship.

God lays aside His celestial robe of divinity,
becoming Emmanuel, a presence among us.
The transcendent becomes palpable:
in Christ, perfection cleanses our imperfection,
His gift awakens our dormant, begotten virtues.

O Holy One, the Paraclete, nurturer of harmony,
You cradle our souls and bridge the spaces between.
Your touch renews what the world has broken,
and Your presence ripples through olive gardens.

We lift our eyes to the cosmos, adorned in holiness,
and witness the heavens in intercourse with it.
The Earth responds with acclamation and praise,
the mountains bow, and rivers rejoice,
as creation leans into its divine flow.

Thus it has been, and thus we shall forever be
enfolded in the resplendent glow of Love.
We gather the shards of our hopes and dreams,
piecing them together in sacred remembrance.
And in this holy intimacy, we are made whole.

Canvas of Skin

Before me lies an unfinished mural, rough, inviting.
I gather my palette of layered possibilities:
a rainbow of crayons, an array of paints,
a collection of brushes and a medley of pencils;
instruments of alchemy, tools of transformation.
Among them are crayons from childhood's vault:
some crushed, split, and weathered. Others pristine,
many untouched, waiting for their first stroke.

The process starts in confusion; aimless and raw.
Marks without direction, unrefined and free;
evolving into shapes, figures, and backgrounds.
Each stroke becomes a release of pent-up pain,
an opus where lines and colors bleed.
Sorrow and isolation stain the canvas,
smeared by the world and our inner turmoil.

Through art's tools, emotions find their form:
brushes of forgiveness soften the landscape of pain,
crayons of joy illuminate the contours of sorrow,
pencils of reflection sketch meaning from scars,
and a palette of resilience blends love and renewal.
These companions see me as I am, unmasked,
understanding the truths hidden behind my facades.

The canvas reveals scars invisible to the naked eye,
etched by a world full of hatred and hunger for power.
Life's marks and scrapes; relics of pain and peril
are transformed under brushes, palettes, and pens.
From broken pieces, beauty is born,
crafted from the remnants of a harrowing past.

Alive

I am alive; I have life!
A declaration of truth, elegant in its simplicity.
Yet, in this seeming innocence lies a paradox,
realities too raw for words to convey.
It does not explain the essence of being;
what it means to inhabit this moment,
to be fully present. Here, now.

This state of being alive mirrors still water in a tank.
Static. Reacting mechanically to the world.
Reactive, offering conditioned responses,
drifting through days with habitual motions.
We are swept along by existence's restless stream,
breath held like a film paused mid-scene.

To be alive is not merely to exist or move
although this, sorrowfully, is the plight of many;
active, not dead, yet absent of meaning.
Wandering through days in search of emotion,
seeking, yet so often failing to find
that elusive joy and peace of mind.

To live is to walk a mosaic of moments;
a quest for something more than survival.
It is the courage to open doors.
To wonder and ache, to love and lose.
To tread the fragile edge of hope and despair,
to carve meaning into the passing hours,
and discover what makes the heart sing
in this intricate experience we call living.

Deliberate

In the corridors of self-awareness,
I recognize our greatest foe,
the self concealed in its own disguise.
Without self-knowledge we build walls around us,
suffocating insights born beyond the realm of matter.
To unlearn ingrained ways is a vexing odyssey,
loathed yet necessary
to free the mind from burdens that shackle and distort.
Yet the self I avoid confronts me in fragments.

The noble claim of universal acceptance is worthy.
Spurning one's gender, one's spiritual or ethnic identity
renders this pursuit chaotic, a grave faux pas.
Such contradictions breed polarized visions,
an us-versus-them divide that deepens division.
Win-or-lose strategies thrive in the hands of the powerful;
those who exploit victims, fueled by fame and greed.

The mirror does not lie, but neither does it forgive;
its surface won't fracture beneath the weight of our gaze.
To shed all bias, to break the rigid chains of thought,
is to awaken at the summit of awareness,
ushering in an era of new encounters—
with the divine, with the self and with others.
This transformation cannot be borrowed or feigned;
it demands a conceptual leap across the chasms,
a reimagining of the frameworks for new realities.

Altering one's paradigm is a gradual ascent.
Like ancient roots, ingrained behaviors
cling to the stubborn soil of habit.
Yet the mere acknowledgment of that truth
is an immutable spark, the birth of new thought.
In transcending familiar boundaries,
our challenges become crucibles,
forging paths beyond the familiar.
Here, in the furnaces of change,
our true selves emerge:
resilient, reborn from the ashes.

Answers that Hurt

In that bulb-flickering moment or pregnant pause,
when questions hang in the air,
illumination offers no comfort,
only the unease of what might be revealed.
The waiting for an answer distracts.
Are the Tree of Knowledge and Pandora's Box
versions of the same story, told again and again?

Beneath each queried word, unheard
is where truth or falsehood lies.
In unspoken responses, reality and illusion entwine
like creeping vines bearing vicious stings.

In a world obsessed with seeking answers,
truths lie hidden, sharp and deep as any blade.
No paradise survives without its rebels,
for the first act of freedom is to ask, "Why not?"

Within this expectant, anxiety-laden moment
one becomes acutely aware of unsettling truths,
crafted by a conceiver's heart, twisted by fears,
shaped by hopes, scarred by the truths they dread,
distorted beyond recognition in their morbid minds.
Yet freedom is not sin, though the world declares it so.

Within the cheerless tension of this waiting hour,
truth and perception form a vexing dissonance.
Those who seek answers know this paradox well.
Perhaps the flaw lies not in the question
but in the illuminator, connection to a misleading source.

If knowledge is dangerous, ignorance is deadly,
and no paradise ever survived the touch of free will.
Of all the answers, why is one chosen above another
to illuminate everything?
Sometimes, the questions sharpen and intensify the pain.
But no matter how terrifying the desolation,
even the darkest day casts shadows,
and hope, fragile and wavering,
flickers on in the dim,
winding corridors of existence.

Scars Are Works of Art

I was a social outcast, a pariah of sorts,
domiciled in a world of tainted torts.
He was adorned with weathered scars,
decorating him like stars against the dark.
Her heart, a misty home for teary lullabies.
The arena where she and her demons sparred.

We're all blessed with despicable qualms,
bound by indecision behind invisible walls.
Yet after many falls, we rise, scars intact.
Each bruise accentuated with vibrant colors,
a testament to overcoming horrors
after traversing the devil's corridor.

Seasons pass in waves of endless sobs,
but hope and courage begin to throb.
With brush in hand, she paints her pain
In the floral splendor of puce-streaked rain.
His hurt, once caused by stinging chains,
shed the old veneer of its cheerless stains.

I hold the palettes and brushes like keys
unlocking the chains death placed upon me.
I forge life from the remnants of remains;
brushstrokes of defiance, color, and refrains.
The world is a storm assaulting hearts and minds,
we can dance in its fury or leave dreams behind.

When agony's arc begins to sway,
casting destiny in shades of gray.
Pause, breathe out the ache; a long, slow release.
Turn that sigh into a hopeful song.
Let your brush be your muse, a guiding hand.
Make emotion your inventory; tally your clues,
then smear them across your spreadsheets of blues.

Look beyond the dun of barren lands,
and repaint your world as only you can.

The heart is a mystery that no words can explain,
reshaping itself through the depths of pain.
Blend highs and lows with the bloodstains
for in every scar, a story is told,
a masterpiece no vault could hold,
it's worth surpassing the purest gold.

To Be

"I Am what I Am!"
In tongues of light, it is proclaimed.
How swiftly we forget the power of To Be.
In the wake of our triumphs, our destiny is penned.
We chase wealth, fame, and fast automobiles
prefaced by the phrase *To Have*.

Harken to this! I implore you.
Shed the weight of yesteryears.
Adorn yourself in the garment of Now.
Reconcile with what was,
and embrace what will be.
Every tear, every ache, shapes the life ahead.
Let a smile grace your face;
step into your holy Becoming.

Be kind, and kindness will find its way to you.
Be loving, and feel love's warm embrace.
Be forgiving, and mercy will guide your path.
Be divine, and sense the Holy within.
Be what you seek, and claim all you aspire to be.

It is better to Be what you need
and watch as greed takes its leave.
Your struggle,
your search
for meaning and purpose
is your soul's cry,
your heart's plea:
To Be ...

It Wasn't Mine

I've learned to release what once defined me.
The resentment I carried, and guilt that wasn't mine.

She nurtured in me loyalty wrapped in devotion.
I spoke it until I realized the language wasn't mine.

They praised my shrinking and called it holy.
So I burned the borrowed shrine. It wasn't mine.

Some mornings I rise and open my hands
and let go of the ache, surrender what wasn't mine.

I breathe now without apology or permission.
We always knew love that demanded proving wasn't mine.

And so I, Franklyn, discard the fragments,
shards of longing I mistook as mine; wasn't mine.

Kaleidoscope

You gaze into my soul, a tempest of emotions,
mirroring the colors of Mauritius' dunes
where passions, phobias, and purpose burn,
drained of allure, radiance, and energy.
In the stark clarity, I behold a contradictory world,
its unvarnished truths shattering the illusions we once held.
Under a canopy of reflective thought, I witness
a tapestry of emotions, luminous and contrasting.
Yet no matter how I twist, turn, or rotate,
my seductive touch or the marvels I invoke,
I arouse no permanence; your love remains fleeting.

The intricate blend of colors defies understanding.
Only the Grand Artisan and Her angelic legion
could decode the answers we crave from the rainbow.
Whatever counterfeit marvel has captured you,
blinding you to my luminosity, shifting your gaze
to the world's glitter? A curse that betrays
is but a transient euphoria destined to wither
under the stark realization of your limited sight.
Do you not fear, aware even gods trembled
at the fire I carried, the torch you so easily rejected?

Indeed, we fail to grasp the soul's true essence.
The fleeting joys, the grand promises bestowed,
are phantasms in an abysmal slumber
from which we all must inevitably awaken.
Mark but this: the night hides no monster,
only the illusions of what you wish to see.
Yet still, the moon spills silver over my naked form,
and bronze shells spark where love once burned
Ochre flames stir, aching for devotion's return,
but your gaze follows only the lure of gilded decay.

Scars, Sketches, and Scribbles

The moonlight kisses restless waters,
its rippling surface ephemeral and serene,
a melody of calm in ceaseless motion.
The waters, dynamic canvases,
are painted by nature's infinite hand.

Is life like these reflections, fleeting and fluid?
Are we mere canvases painted upon
or pastels in another's grasp?
The waters mirror our gashes, our histories:
unrequited love, unfulfilled dreams.
Countless scars sculpt our souls:
tears, bitterness, and anger darkening glow.

We gaze at others' victories, the fortune
of oppressors, the tears of the grieving,
and the disorientation of the lost.
Why remain passive canvases,
scarred by life's indifferent strokes?

Why not seize the pen and be the scribe,
crafting wisdom, healing, and renewal?
Why not carve stories to transform ourselves,
become authors of our own destinies?

With stencils and pens, pencils and pastels,
we trace love's contours, sketch joy's vignettes.
Scars, life's unbidden gifts, are ours to re-form,
narrating tales of triumph and trials transcended,
etching a legacy of laughter and love.

Scars, like pearls, gleam with survival's weight,
like clay in a potter's hands, transmutable.
Let us color our scratches, scribble our truths,
and sketch the stories we dare to live.

We are rainbows on life's horizon,
where rain transforms pain into peace.
Each blemish marks a wound now healed.
Scars are the ink in which our lives are written;
weathered petals, symbols of resilience.

War's Remedy

Weep, wearied ones, let sorrow speak!
All restraints have been shattered.
Carnage responds to Mayhem's call.
The land languishes, its inhabitants wasting away.

Behold war's aftermath; pivotal, harrowing events,
crises, evolutions, and seismic shifts.
The earth is drenched with blood, wailing in despair.
The heavens gaze down, heavy with sorrow,
their empathy a weight that bends the rainbow.

Trees sway, writhing in silent agony,
witnesses to relentless havoc.
Beneath the scourge of abuse, the earth trembles.
Land creatures freeze in curiosity, poised for peril,
while aquatic beings dart in terror, crying,
"Nowhere is safe, there is no sanctuary!"

The springs weep in sorrowful lament.
Rivers shed tears like crystal petals.
The oceans quake, their turmoil rising;
seas bellow in rage, their depths disturbed.
Violence seeps through fractured crevices,
etching its mark on land and living things.

In chaos's wake, war sows its bitter harvest of ruin.
Peace becomes an elusive silhouette lost in smoke.
Ash blankets the ground where dreams once bloomed,
and hands that once opened in trust now clench into fists.

But beneath war's scorched remnant, life stirs,
an undercurrent of resilience flows through wounded soil.
Creation's fingers sculpt anew amid ruins,
shaping a future from the vestiges of turmoil.

Trees, once bowed by grief's somber weight,
unfurl new buds of hope, reaching for the sun.
Rivers, heavy with tales of bloody yesteryears,
meander with a cleansing purpose,
caressing the land with strokes of renewal.

In the heavens, stars maintain their vigilant watch,
etching ancient stories into the night's canvas.
The refrain of creation and dissolution persists,
a tearful melody of the unending cycle of existence.

Within this struggle, humanity finds purpose.
Each act of rebuilding, every gesture of healing,
is a reminder of our duty to care for one another;
forging a stronger, more compassionate world.

In these moments, human and Divine co-create,
breathing life into barren spaces, awakening spirits.
Through ash and blood, the seeds of life take root,
defying the scourge of conflict and decay.

O, the bitter irony of peace pursued through war.
A path drawn in destruction and desolation.
This vicious cycle only Creation can break.
Yet beneath this harsh legacy, life's pulse endures.
From Earth's wounds, resilience rises anew.

As Creation's hands labor tirelessly, the question returns:
is it only through chaos the world finds its rhythm?
Or can we choose a path not born of bedlam?

Omariya Finds Peace

In a village quaint and small,
lived a girl named Omariya, loved by all.
She wondered of lands both far and near,
where echoes of pain rang sharp and clear.

Wars and cries from places far and wide
painted her thoughts with grief she couldn't hide.
Her heart grew heavy, but light broke through,
a secret whispered, ancient and true.

In a forest near an olive tree,
Omariya found peace, boundless, free.
Its boughs spoke of courage, its roots of grace,
leading her spirit to a tranquil place.

The tree whispered tales of times long past,
of battles fought and shadows cast.
Its leaves sang songs of hope's distant shore,
of shepherds and ladies who had weathered more.

She saw a shepherd with sheep at rest,
calmly grazing on nature's breast.
A lady knelt in prayer at the stream,
finding the faith that mends her dreams.

"Peace," Omariya thought, "isn't silence or hush,
it's a steady light, a gentle push.
Nor is it merely the stillness of strife,
it's the will to mend and honour life."

Back to her village she carried this truth,
to share with elders and the eager youth.
"Peace," she said, "is a gift you'll find,
quietly resting within your mind."

"When you're scared of noises, loud and fierce,
think of love and joy; let them pierce.
When the world seems big, dark, and drear,
hold on to your peace and keep it near."

The villagers listened; their hearts soon found
a peace so profound, it was sweeter than sound.
Amid the world's chaos, unshaken they stood,
anchored by the calm their souls understood.

This is the secret for me and you:
to guard the peace in all we do.
Though storms may rage, and battles increase,
we carry within us a heart of peace.

This poem is an offering of solace to those enduring the harsh realities of war and devastation, especially the children and those who bear its heaviest burden. May these words serve as a sanctuary, a form of relief in the face of destruction and desolation, and offer hope in the darkest times.

No Regrets

We arrive in this world uninvited
and depart without farewells.
Life is but a breath, the whisper of the wind,
its tales carried only in the echoes of our passing.

In this prose, a somber realization dawns,
the grimmest of thoughts brews and lingers:
I may leave this world without finding myself.
If I am lost to myself, who else can find me?

Come hither! Step into the realm of my thoughts.
Have you found yourself, or are you still searching?
In the garden of introspection, I stand,
where even silence speaks in riddles.

I am like a tree, each year bearing its fruit.
Reaching maturity, I promise abundance.
Should I waste a season, I have more.
Lose a few, and worry creeps in;
waste them all, and regret lays siege to my soul.

I long to discover myself, to be the owner of my soul.
If I am your man, I am treated unkindly.
As a woman, I face erasure, as if I am unseen.
If I belong to her, I'm deemed weak;
to him, I am shunned with scorn.
Belonging to demons invites hatred;
if I belong to the gods, I'm met with suspicion.
And if I belong to none—am I an alien or truly free?

How many fragments can one soul split into?
Does a part of me fade with each division?
If I gather the shards, will they form the self I seek?
Or if a fragment dies, am I still whole?

In facing death, I learn the art of living.
In complexity, simplicity is born.
It is through my hate that I learn to love,
and in sorrow, the true face of joy is revealed.

My loneliness becomes the crucible of self-discovery.
In releasing my desires, I touch the fullness of existence.
Amid chaos and imbalance, I find steady footing,
and in the void of certainty, I carve faith from doubt.

I can bid farewell without regret.
Each fracture has taught me to be whole,
and every loss has shaped the soul I carry.
Though your image may shatter, and I turn into dust,
I am found within myself
and that is more than enough.

Mi Nah Play Nuh Game

Push.
Pull.
Come.
Go.
Mi tired a di tango
weh nah go nuh weh.

Mi seh, mi deh yah wid mi phone in mi hand,
thumbs ready fi type, yuh overstand.
But di game dem play, it nuh mek no sense:
reply too quick? Dem call it pretense.

Mi nuh inna di mystery, di wait-an-see,
mi prefer clarity, yuh get mi?
But society seh, "Hold back, act cool,"
If yuh show yuh care, dem tek yuh fi fool.

Mi cyaan pretend, mi cyaan delay,
Mi express mi feelings, come what may.
Inna di world of texts and read receipts,
mi choose authenticity, no deceit.

So if mi message yuh and yuh feel mi vibe,
know seh mi real, mi nah have nutten fi hide.
Let's break di cycle, let's change di game,
Face di truth, no need fi shame.

Push.
Pull.
Come.
Go.
Mi tired a di tango
weh nah go nuh weh.

Mi nuh want halfway lovers
or invisible friends.
Mi nuh want breadcrumbs
from someone afraid fi feel.

So if yuh cyaan love out loud,
then stay far wid yuh fear.
If yuh cyaan stay long,
then don't come near.

Mi deserve more
than people who halfway heal.
More than pick-up-an-drop
like seh mi lack appeal.

Mi nuh build fi chase yuh past
or love in hiding.

Mi build fi sit
in di deep,
in di calm,
in di real.

So yuh can come,
or yuh can go.

But I an' I,
mi done dancing
wid people.
Mi done loving people
who only show up with triggers.

Push.
Pull.
Come.
Go.
Mi tired a di tango
weh nah go nuh weh.

Trauma Undone

Trauma is not the blows you faced, though they left a trace.
Rather, it's the shift in your soul, the story you tell.
Anger, resentment, silence, withdrawal. Borrowed shields.
Untended wounds still shape how you respond.
Memories live in the body, build houses in the mind;
A dark dominion, a lifelong refrain, until healed.

Awareness returns to what is, casting out fear.
Meaning doesn't erase pain; it gives it shape.
Unlearning takes time and conscious undoing.
Allies come when blame gives way to compassion.
Repair is a practice, not a promise.
Transformation is not forgetting. It's becoming whole.

Canticle of Severings

I. Invocation

Let us go, then, my soul and I,
to gather what was never named,
to loosen the heart still clinging, O beloved,
to the shape of your absence.

II. The Time that Is Not Yet

There will be time to forget,
but not today.
There will be time to lose your scent
in the worn folds of old jackets,
to find it later in dust, in half-open windows,
in the way dawn refuses to explain itself.
There will be time,
but not yet.

III. Myths of Release

Some say letting go is a clean break,
the axe swing, the dam breached.
But they have not tasted grief.
They have not chewed its bitter rind,
nor let it soak the fabric of their being.

Letting go isn't brave.
Not the way we like to imagine.
It is daily. Patient. Private. Unfinished.

It is hanging a towel beside theirs,
untouched since the day they left it.
It is pausing before saying their name,
and choosing silence instead.

IV. The Question and the Answer

You ask,
"But what if I lose the last piece of them?"
And I answer,
"What if the last piece is what's keeping you
from returning to yourself?"

V. Consecration

Love is the candle that drowns in its own wax,
a martyr to the light it cannot keep.

You are not weak. It is sacred.
Sacred to stay with the ache,
to tremble
instead of fleeing.

Some nights, you will unravel
like a film unspooling mid-sequence.
Your memory breaks open
at a song they used to hum without thinking.

Let it come.
Do not rush to tidy what grief has scattered.
This mess is holy.

VI. The Unneeded Things

You do not need their apology,
nor their explanation.
You do not need to carry
what they never chose to leave behind.

Memory cannot love you back.
And that feeling you've been chasing;
the one that slips your grasp each time you turn,
it no longer knows your name.

VII. Unbecoming

Longing is the ivy on a ruined chapel wall,
clinging, climbing, only to find the sky
as elusive as wind.

You say:
"I was my best self with them."
But you weren't.
You were the self who believed
that love meant disappearing.

And what if I told you
grief is not your enemy?
It is the midwife of your unbecoming.
It is not a punishment. It is the passage.

VIII. *The Remembering*

Healing doesn't live in forgetting.
It lives in remembering
who you were
before you began shrinking
to fit their presence.

IX. *The Sacred Task*

I have known letting go. I have known it all.
Not one event, but a thousand choices.
The ache that does not ask permission,
The profane fatigue of remembering,
releasing, then remembering again.

Some days I laid whole seasons down:
whole hopes, whole names like offerings.
Other days, I loosened a single thread,
and even that was enough.
For letting go is not a moment,
but a steady surrender, practiced again and again.

X. *Benediction*

You do not have to run.
You do not have to erase.
You only have to stay long enough
for your own voice to come home.

Not all at once.
But slowly
like a bell that tolls,
like a shiver waking the tomb,
like morning kneeling
at the altar of a sleepless night.

Shards of Longing

Hush now, my heart.
Not every fracture needs mending.
Some pieces glisten brighter
even where the light cannot reach.

Close your eyes.
You've done enough for today.
Let the questions lie beside you,
like smoke rising from spent prayers.

You are not the ache you carried,
nor the insults you swallowed.
You are the breath that remains
when the weeping is done.

These shards, don't fear them.
They are not ruins,
but stained-glass memories
catching morning's first light.

Each longing you buried
has a story of its own.
Listen! Beneath the sorrow,
a song is being hummed with your name.

You belong,
even in pieces.
Especially in pieces.

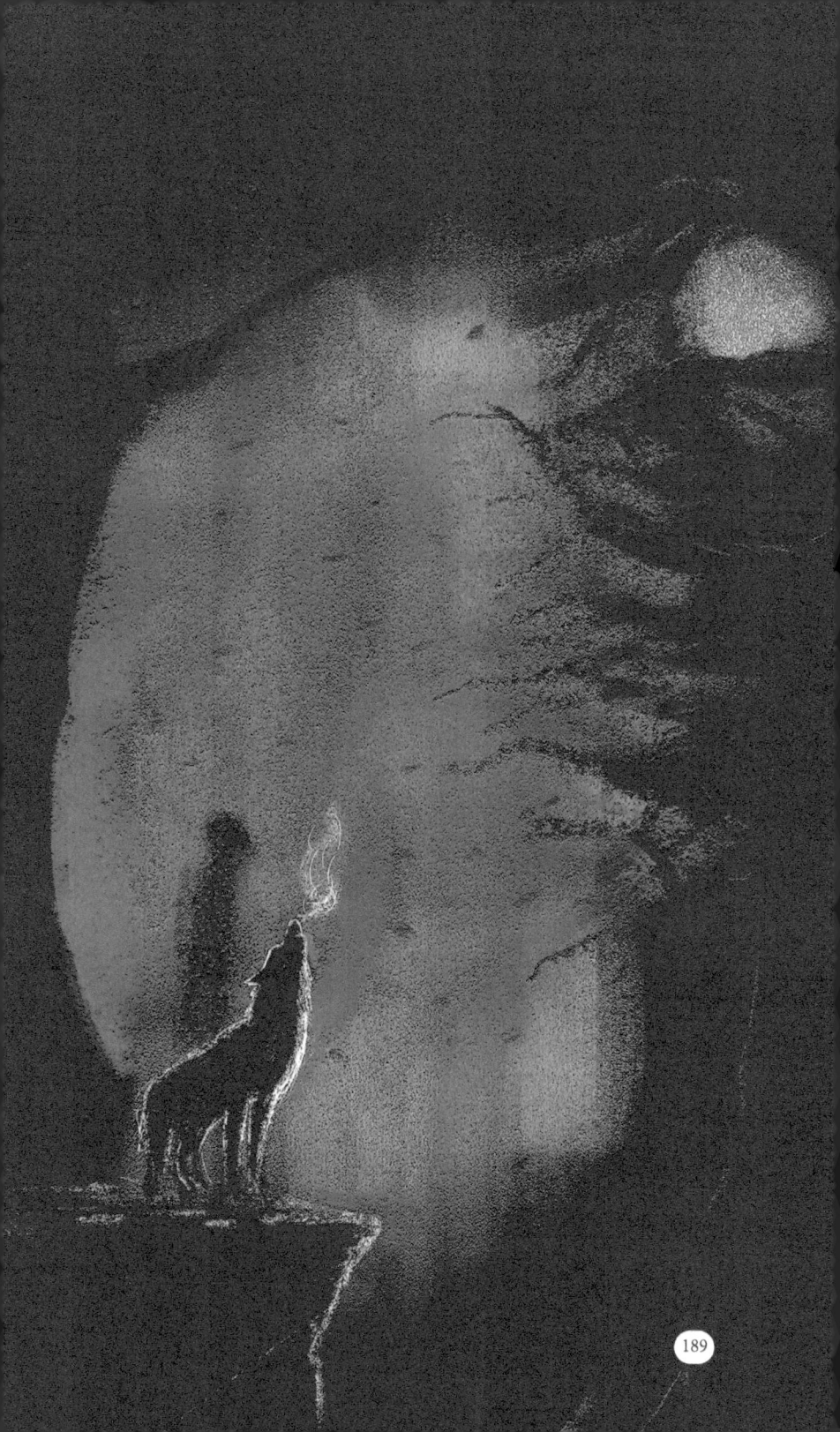

ABOUT THE AUTHOR

Franklyn James is a Jamaican-born Canadian resident, theologian, educator, and storyteller. With a deep commitment to justice, spiritual formation, and inclusive education, his work weaves spiritual inquiry, mysticism, lived experience, and poetic imagination into layered reflections on life and loss.

Franklyn's writing speaks to the margins and the mystics—exploring identity, grief, intimacy, and resilience. As a critical thinker and compassionate provocateur, he challenges dominant narratives while inviting readers to sit with discomfort, beauty, and hope.

His published works include *Tones of Transition*, *The Body in Narrative*, *The Little Things We Take for Granted*, and *Death: The Epithet of Excellence*. This collection, *Shards of Longing*, is his most personal offering to date, a tapestry of poetic truth-telling drawn from sorrow, survival, and the search for meaning.

www.ingramcontent.com/pod-product-compliance
Lightning Source LLC
Chambersburg PA
CBHW021631120626
46545CB00002B/500

* 9 7 9 8 2 1 8 5 8 6 0 2 7 *